Growth, Development and Welfare

Growth, Development and Welfare

An Essay on Levels of Living

Ajit K. Dasgupta

Basil Blackwell

British Library Cataloguing in Publication Data
Dasgupta, Ajit K. (Ajit Kumar)
  Growth, development and welfare.
  1. Economic development – Sociological
  perspectives
  I. Title
  306'.3

  ISBN 0–631–14399–8

Library of Congress Cataloging in Publication Data
Dasgupta, Ajit Kumar,
  Growth, development, and welfare / Ajit K. Dasgupta.
    p.   cm.
  Bibliography: p.
  Includes index.
  ISBN 0–631–14399–8
  1. Economic development.   2. Welfare economics.   I. Title.
HD82.D3165 1988
338.9—dc19   87–36564 CIP

Typeset in 11 on 13 pt Bembo
by Columns of Reading
Printed in Great Britain by TJ Press, Padstow

Contents

Tables

In memory of my parents

Acknowledgements

I am grateful for comments on an earlier draft, or discussion of specific points, to Robin Ghosh, Peter Henderson, Nola Leov, Priyatosh Maitra, John Parker, Roy Perett and Monimoy Sen, and to an anonymous reviewer. On some topics discussed in this book, I have learnt over the years from my students in Calcutta, Southampton, Montreal, Delhi, Melbourne, Canberra and Dunedin. Some of the contents of chapters 1 and 2 have been presented earlier, as part of an inaugural lecture at the University of Otago in 1984 and at a seminar at the National Development Studies Centre, Australian National University in 1985. I am grateful to Maud Boock for typing numerous drafts of the manuscript with patience and precision. Lastly, thanks are due to my wife and daughter for their cooperation with this enterprise.

Introduction

'Political economist', notes an historian, was used as a swear-word in England of the 1830s to denote an enemy of the common people.[1] In the period since, economics has advanced greatly as a discipline, but its practitioners are yet far from being generally acclaimed as friends of humanity.

Perhaps the most important reason for the distrust of economics is widespread acceptance of the view that economic growth (an increase in the gross national product or GNP) does not 'really' make people better off. Dissatisfaction with GNP as an index of social welfare has led to a search for other measures. Some have attempted to adjust ('correct') the GNP measure itself to take such things as leisure and environmental pollution into account.[2] Others have developed 'physical' (i.e. 'non-monetary') indices, described as 'social indicators', which are usually intended as supplements to the GNP measure for evaluating social states, but sometimes as substitutes for GNP.[3] While *statistical* issues involved in the use of social indicators to evaluate social wellbeing have received considerable attention, basic *conceptual* issues have not. The use of GNP as a measure of social welfare rests ultimately on the notion of desire fulfilment for individuals. Does the same notion underlie indicators other than GNP? If not, what other principles could reasonably be used for justifying their use? How far do specific social indicators (the rate of literacy and the expectation of life at birth in particular) satisfy these principles? In practice, do rankings of social states by the GNP criterion and by other criteria give identical results? It is

1

questions such as these to which the core of this book (namely chapters 3 to 5) is addressed.

The first two chapters are concerned in a more direct way with certain misgivings that have often been expressed about standard economic theory, of which one has already been mentioned; namely, that a higher real income may not lead to increased welfare because, for instance, people are not made any happier by a higher material standard of living.

Yet another charge against economics is its narrow vision of what governs human action. Rational economic man, it is said, is concerned only with self-interest, but not so real men, who are also moved to action by a variety of other motives, such as sympathy, benevolence, charity, envy, malice, patriotism and power. Hence, it is argued, most of human behaviour may be outside the scope of economic analysis.

Economists are also vulnerable to the charge of being biased in favour of the capitalist order. Such a bias, it is said, has been inherent in economic theory since its early beginnings in the writings of Adam Smith. The bias is evident, so runs the argument, from the fact that the system of 'free enterprise' (or 'laissez-faire'), which is taken to mean a system based on private ownership of the means of production and the allocation of resources through the market, has been regarded by economists not simply as a particular, even perhaps a passing, phase in history, but as providing a normative standard in terms of which all other forms of society are to be judged. This, it is claimed, has had the consequence of making the main body of economic theory biased against economic systems other than capitalism and in particular against socialist economic systems.

Finally, a persistent charge against economic theory has been its lack of curiosity about the origin of preference orderings. The economist takes individual preferences as given, but does not enquire how preferences came to be, what they are. This, it has been argued by some, makes economic theory seriously incomplete. In particular, the failure to take the *social* origins of individual preferences into account has been held to make the evaluation of social states by a preference-satisfaction criterion invalid.

These alleged defects of the economic approach have a bearing on several issues that arise in comparing the level of wellbeing of one society with that of another, whether such comparison is done on the basis of GNP or something else. For this reason, an examination of the 'charges' described is attempted in chapters 1 and 2.

A broad outline of topics discussed in various chapters of this book is provided below. Chapter 1 begins by considering some recent claims based on the interpretation of survey data on self-rated happiness, that material prosperity does *not* make people feel better off. The next section goes on to ask in what sense, if any, economic theory is committed to the doctrine of laissez-faire. The fundamental notions of individual preference and choice and their relationship to that of self-interest are discussed in section 1.3. The chapter concludes with a look at the kind of relationship that economic theory postulates between economic and non-economic aspects of welfare.

Chapter 2 consists of three sections. The first examines in what sense individual preferences can be said to be socially influenced or determined, and corresponding implications for the concept and measurement of social wellbeing. Section 2.2 criticizes some doctrines of socio-cultural determinism as applied to the Third World. The last section considers some possible effects of economic growth on culture.

Chapter 3 distinguishes between four principles on the basis of which the use of social indicators for evaluating social states could be justified, namely individual preference, basic needs, rights and excellence, and looks also at relationships *between* the principles. Among the issues that receive special attention in this chapter are the distinctions between 'relative' and 'absolute' concepts of deprivation and between 'positive' and 'negative' rights. The question whether 'nationalist' goals merit any special consideration when evaluating the level of wellbeing of a society is also addressed.

Chapter 4 takes up two particular types of indicators, namely the literacy rate and demographic indices (including the infant mortality rate and the expectation of life at birth) for special attention and seeks to find what rationale, if any, they might have in terms of the basic principles set out in previous chapters.

Chapter 5 consists largely of statistical analysis. Section 5.1 sets out the basic data, which are then used to analyse comparative levels of living in some developing countries, using such indicators as the literacy rate and the expectation of life at birth, as well as per capita GNP. The extent to which levels of living in these countries have improved since the 1960s is discussed in the next section. Both in comparing levels of living and in comparing changes in these levels, particular attention is paid to the question of how far comparisons made in terms of the social indicators chosen lead to the same conclusions as those based on per capita GNP. Section 5.3 looks briefly at changes in levels of living which occurred in some European countries during the Industrial Revolution and also compares the statistical record of growth and development in Europe in that period with the record of developing countries in the recent past. The chapter, and the book, concludes with a few general remarks.

1
Economic Growth and Welfare

Think about prospective actions, testing them with questions like
'How do I profit if I do it and how, if I don't', and then do it or
don't.

Mahābhārata

Can't move 'em with a cold thing like economics.

Ezra Pound, *The Pisan Cantos*

This chapter is concerned with certain criticisms that have often
been levelled against the economic approach to the evaluation of
social states. It consists of four sections. The first examines some
recent claims, made on the basis of survey date on self-rated
happiness, to the effect that material prosperity does *not* make
people feel better off. Section 1.2 asks the question whether
economic theory provides any warrant for the doctrine of laissez-
faire. Section 1.3 discusses the notions of preference, welfare and
choice for individuals and the relationship of these to the concept
of self-interest. The last section looks at how economic and non-
economic aspects of welfare are related.

1.1 Economic Growth and Happiness: The Interpretation of Survey Data

The view that growth in incomes, or more generally, material
prosperity, would not really make people feel happier or 'better
off' has been stated from ancient times, and in many different
societies. But it is only recently that such views have been sought
to be substantiated on the basis of quantitative studies. We begin
by considering an argument of this kind, based on data provided
by surveys on self-rated happiness, that has attracted a certain
amount of attention.[1] According to this argument, while
economists may indeed have argued in favour of economic
growth because of their belief that this would help achieve

5

greater wellbeing, the belief itself is mistaken.

In the survey by Cantril, a large number of people in different countries were asked to state their economic, and other, aspirations. The contrast in particular between statements by Indian and American consumers has drawn much comment. Among Indian respondents, one mentioned decent food and clothing; another a bicycle, a fan and a radio; yet another 'better clothing for my wife', a cow for milk and ghee, a piece of land and 'to construct a house of my own'. Among the Americans a new car is frequently mentioned. One would like as well better furniture and more vacations; another a house, a boat and 'sending my four children to private schools' while a third aspires to music and dancing lessons for the children and belonging to a country club. Cantril concludes that aspiration levels of people from less developed countries tend to be modest as compared to those from highly developed countries.[2] Easterlin's study, which is partly based on the same data, has a slightly different emphasis, namely that tastes are a product of 'socialization experience', a proposition which, he states, is well accepted by social scientists 'other than economists'.[3] Moreover, the nature of this 'socialization' is such that tastes shift 'upwards' with development, offsetting 'the positive effect of income growth on wellbeing that one would expect on the basis of economic theory'.[4] The implication clearly is that efforts to improve human welfare in poor countries by means of economic development are futile.

The interpretation that Cantril and Easterlin (and some others) have put on the responses recorded in the survey fails to distinguish between a change of taste, an increase in knowledge and a rise in income. In consequence, their argument treats as a difference in tastes what is more naturally regarded as a difference in opportunities open to the agents concerned. The economic theory of consumer's choice helps one sort out two distinct reasons which may lead to a particular combination of goods *not* being purchased: first because the consumer may not be able to afford it, given his income and the prices facing him, and secondly because, even though he could afford it, some other affordable combination ranks higher in his preference ordering ('tastes'). The goods mentioned by the consumers surveyed by

Cantril clearly belong to the first category. But there are many such goods. The ones mentioned are naturally taken to be those that the consumer could afford were his income a little higher than it is; they represent local, not global, aspiration levels.[5] What the difference in the stated aspiration levels shows therefore, is that most consumers in developed countries have greater economic opportunities open to them; hardly a surprising result, since this is the reason for calling such countries developed.

This interpretation finds further support from two other considerations, namely first, few of the items mentioned by American consumers are unknown to people in less developed areas ('who have not yet learned all that is potentially available to people in more advanced societies'),[6] the discreet pleasures of belonging to a country club being a possible exception; and secondly, economic concerns are the category of personal hopes related to happiness most frequently mentioned by the consumers surveyed.

Cantril's results are based largely on answers by respondents to hypothetical questions about their aspiration levels, i.e. about desired future consumption. People can also be asked directly whether they think they are better or worse off now as compared to some time or times in the recent past. This has been done in a number of country-specific, and sometimes group-specific, studies in Western Europe, Japan and some of the less developed countries. A typical finding is that reported by Harrison[7] for Britain, namely that older working-class people looking back on the 1950s from the vantage point of the 1970s stressed the positive gains which affluence had brought through increased comfort and freedom: 'They had no doubts at all about the great benefits brought by washing machines and hot water systems.'

We conclude with two observations of a more general nature. One is that poor people, the world over, if asked about their aspirations, have usually been found to 'play it cool'. This has often been taken by 'social scientists other than economists' to indicate the low level of aspiration of the people concerned. Our discussion should have made it clear that this interpretation could be misleading. Secondly, socialization *does* influence an individual's preferences and we shall consider later in this chapter the relevance of this in comparing standards of living as between different societies, but it does not do so in quite such a mechanical way as some have supposed. It is one thing to recognize the social context of preferences and quite another to insist that they must change with consumption in such a way that a consumer who has greater income and hence can now afford to buy more of the things he originally preferred, can never be made better off thereby. If for example economic progress enables the 'average' Indian to better fulfil such present desires as those for decent food, improved housing and better clothing for his wife, to argue that this would not 'really' make him better off, because in the process he may have acquired a different set of desires, does not appear terribly convincing. The 'optimistic' beliefs of economists seem to be better grounded in common sense, after all.

1.2 Economics and Laissez-faire

We now turn to another question; in what sense, if any, can economics be said to be committed to 'laissez-faire'? 'Laissez-faire' itself has been given a variety of meanings by historians, political scientists and economists.[8] In the context of economic analysis, it has usually been taken to refer to a state of affairs in which the allocation of resources is made by the market mechanism and the State does not intervene in the economy, except to the extent necessary for preserving law and order. It has been said that laissez-faire in this sense does not and cannot exist, so that arguing about its merits is a bit like arguing about those of unicorns. This is a superficial view. Laissez-faire (like perfect competition) could be regarded as a 'limiting' or 'ideal type' state of affairs to which actual situations may be judged to be approximately close, or from which they are far, as the case may be. Hence a minimalist conception of the activities of the State is not necessarily without substantive content, and it has in fact exercised considerable influence on economic policy. In that context, it has been interpreted in a normative way, namely as a recommendation that the State should *not* extend its activities beyond those of a nightwatchman, and the scale and nature of economic activities should be determined by the market. And it is often supposed that such a view is justified by economic theory.

It is natural to start this account by mentioning Adam Smith's *The Wealth of Nations*, which has usually been interpreted as a celebration of the market mechanism. Smith did provide in that book powerful and cogent arguments against various kinds of intervention in the economy that governments of his day were wont to indulge in. His arguments were successful. They contributed towards bringing about a situation where a more restricted role of the government in economic affairs came to be regarded as both normal and appropriate. They may also help explain why a presumption in favour of decentralized mechanisms of resource allocation came, in time, to be accepted as part of the received doctrine of economics. Yet to regard Adam Smith primarily as an apostle of the 'free market' system, and a fortiori, to see in his writing the original sin (or virtue) of economics is to miss the point. First, as Viner pointed out in a classic essay,[9] Smith did *not* address the question of government versus markets in the abstract. His attack was against unreasonable regulations enforced and excessive power enjoyed by governments of his day, in particular that of his own country. The system of 'natural liberty' that Smith favoured consisted of four basic elements, namely the free choice of occupations, free trade in land, internal free trade and free foreign trade. None of these could be found in British society of his time but they could all be achieved by appropriate reforms to existing regulations. The free choice of occupations required the abolition of apprenticeship regulations and of settlement laws. Free trade in land could be achieved by repealing the prevailing system of entails, primogeniture and other such regulations. Free trade in domestic markets was even easier to achieve; all that was needed was the abolition of local customs taxes, while free foreign trade required not only the abolition of import duties and export subsidies, but also an end to trading monopolies of chartered companies, such as the East India Company.

According to Smith, what functions were proper for a government to carry out depended in part on its standards of honesty and competence. Where good administration was available as in Venice and Amsterdam, Smith would allow mercantile projects to be included among the appropriate functions of government. The government of England, however, which tended to conduct itself in peacetime with 'slothful and negligent profusion', could not be trusted safely with such projects.

None of this means that the view of Smith as an anti-interventionist is false. However liberally his definition of the 'duties of the sovereign' is interpreted – the 'duty of establishing an *exact* administration of justice',[10] in particular, could include a great deal – he was clearly against regular and wide-ranging intervention by the government in normal economic activities, for he believed that given a measure of competition, and provided the general tendency of society towards progress was not rendered ineffective by special circumstances, individual enterprise, by and large, could do a better job. But our discussion above does suggest that for Smith both markets and governments were merely means. The end was the wealth of nations, i.e. material progress, and all that this could contribute towards making individual development for the masses of the people not only possible, but practically attainable, in the not too distant future. The logic of Smith's writing still works powerfully against regarding state control of industry as a remedy for economic ills, but it works no less against ideologies of the right, which value markets *as such*, and would regard the implementation of market-based decisions as the supreme end of public policy, irrespective either of circumstances or of human consequences involved. Smith 'did not believe that laissez-faire was always good or always bad. It depended on circumstances' (Viner, p. 155). And contemporary welfare economics has also come closer to such a view than is often realized.

Stated in the terminology of welfare economics, the question we have been discussing can be said to turn on the optimality properties of a competitive equilibrium. Under certain conditions, including the absence of externalities in production and in consumption, a competitive equilibrium has been shown to be a Pareto optimum, i.e. a state such that given production technology and consumers' preferences, no person could be made better off without someone else being made worse off.

This does not, however, commit the economist to a view of competitive equilibrium as being socially optimal. A competitive equilibrium, even if it is a Pareto optimum, may involve a more unequal income distribution than is regarded as acceptable from a social point of view. The theory of welfare economics does *not* tell us that a competitive equilibrium based on any given initial distribution of endowments will lead to a distribution of incomes that is more reasonable, fair or just, that gives rise to greater aggregate social welfare and so on, as compared to other possible distributions. The concept of a Pareto optimum, which is all that the theorem asserts a competitive equilibrium to be, does not allow of such considerations. Confusion about this point is largely due to misleading terminology. As Koopmans pointed out long ago, the expression Pareto 'optimum' is a misnomer. What it denotes is allocative efficiency.[11] Even so, the theorem referred to, namely that a competitive equilibrium is a Pareto optimum, is much less than a claim about the efficiency of capitalism. We would first have to be satisfied that an actual real-life capitalist economy is sufficiently similar to a competitive equilibrium for the theorem to apply.

'Perfect competition' requires a number of very stringent conditions which are such that they cannot be exactly realized in practice by any social organization, but for the theorem as stated to have a cutting edge, it must be possible to decide whether or not they are approximately realized. This cannot itself be a matter of theory. It is a matter of judgement. We must judge whether some actual set of institutions provides such a large number of so very well-organized markets that these institutions are sufficiently close to perfect competition to have comparable efficiency.[12] Many actual economies of a generally 'capitalist' kind (i.e. based on the private property in the means of production and using markets rather than direct controls by the State as the principal means of resource allocation) may well be judged to be not so close to perfect competition in the relevant sense after all.

The Pareto optimality of perfect competition cannot then be used as a basis for making inferences about the efficiency or otherwise of such economies. The theorems of welfare economics are also not tied to the capitalist system. We have the following 'converse theorem'; under certain conditions a Pareto optimum is a competitive equilibrium. A socialist economy which, let us suppose, has brought about a radical redistribution in assets and income but wishes to maintain the efficiency of the resulting, particular, Pareto optimal outcome associated with this distribution, may well find the 'converse' theorem both interesting and useful.

Economists with socialist leanings, notably Lange and Lerner, were among the first to establish mathematical relationships between the pricing mechanism and optimal allocation of resources in a socialist economy. In his classic analysis of the relationship of competitive equilibrium to Pareto optimality, Koopmans not only refers to this work, but he takes care to point out that discussion of price criteria in this context does not necessarily pre-suppose the existence of a competitive market organization on capitalist lines and that pricing as a tool for planning and operating a socialist economy is a perfectly acceptable interpretation of the same theorems. That such criteria have *not* been greatly favoured for resource allocation in the Soviet economy is probably due more to Russian history than the logic of socialism, and the current Chinese preoccupation with prices and markets, far from being an aberration, is best seen as a return to a long-standing socialist tradition. Opponents of such policies have indeed predicted that they will inevitably lead to the re-establishment of capitalism in China but this, in my judgement, is extremely unlikely, however cunning history's passages might be.

The belief that support for market-oriented policies necessarily constitutes support for capitalism is widespread and this fact has considerable political importance, but the belief itself is mistaken. Enthusiasm about the converse theorem providing a blue-print for socialism must, however, be moderated by the following considerations. First, the problem of identification, i.e. of arriving at a judgement on what, in practice, constitutes a sufficiently close approximation to a 'competitive equilibrium' remains just as important here as in the previous case. Secondly, the theorem only holds under special assumptions. it does not apply to goods involving externalities, for which an allocation based on prices would fail to be Pareto-optimal, nor to 'public goods',[13] such as clean air, which being both non-excludable in supply and non-rival in consumption, cannot be split up and sold in individual lots, and for which, in consequence, markets are usually impossible; and it breaks down under economies of scale. Thirdly, there is the problem of ensuring adequate incentives. Some types of incentives are taken care of by the price mechanism itself. But there are others. The attempt to achieve a social optimum necessarily involves a fundamental incentive problem in the following sense. Social welfare, which by hypothesis it is the aim of planning to maximize, depends on the consumers' preferences and their endowments. Eliciting this information involves an incentive problem. People may lack incentive to reveal such information to 'society' in order that the right ('optimal') initial distribution could be determined.[14] Indeed, they could have an incentive to mislead, by overstating wants (or needs) and understating productive ability. In some form or other this problem ('incentive compatibility') has been long recognized.

Thus, commenting on the programme 'from each according to his ability, to each according to his need', which Marx and Engels said in the *Communist Manifesto* a socialist society would inscribe on its banner, Proudhon pointed out the following difficulty: 'You say that my need is 90 and my ability 100: I maintain that my need is 100 and my ability 90.' Implementing the programme required knowledge of the numbers but the relevant knowledge may not be conveyed by price signals alone. The difficulty exists, in principle, in any form of society, and could apply to private as well as public goods.

Yet perhaps the authors of the *Manifesto* were not quite so careless as Proudhon thought. How important a problem incentive compatibility is in practice will surely be affected by individuals' perceptions about the nature of the society in which they live. The Marxian principle was intended to apply only in a society in which 'the free development of all is the condition for the free development of each'. If individuals perceive their society as being truly such (or even as one with a decent chance of becoming such) their motivation for mis-statement (even in terms of self-interested preferences) could disappear.[15] We are still very far from realizing such a state of affairs!

Summing up the virtue of competitive equilibrium lies essentially in allocational efficiency resulting from the economy of information. Recent work has brought out that such economy may not be quite as far-reaching, hence the advantage not quite as decisive, as previously thought; for non-price considerations relating to incentives, authority and motivation could be relevant as well. Nevertheless, over wide areas of economic activity, the case for decentralized decision making remains a powerful one. This case finds a certain measure of support from our two theorems on the relationship between a competitive equilibrium and a pareto optimum. In particular they tell us that publicly owned industry with decentralized price-based decision making could well provide an efficient allocation of resources while privately owned industry subject to a plethora of administrative direct controls could be grossly inefficient. However, such considerations could, in practice, be given their due without necessarily invoking general equilibrium theorems, such as those cited above on the relationship between a competitive equilibrium and Pareto optimality, at all.[16] The observed rigidity of centralized decision processes, their inability to take changing circumstances into account quickly enough, is particularly relevant here. It has also been observed that certain forms of centralization in decision making tend to cause much more damage than others. This is a matter of much practical importance on which received theory offers little guidance, and one where a 'second best' approach seems more appropriate.[17]

The question of the welfare implications of free markets, as opposed to State intervention, could also be addressed in a different way. There can be few economies which have relied entirely on free markets, or entirely on the State, for allocating resources, but the relative importance of one vis-à-vis the other has varied widely. Therefore, by looking at how various economies have actually performed in terms of per capita GNP, or some other indicator of social welfare, we could try to establish whether or not free markets may be regarded prima facie as promoting welfare. Such an approach involves a basic problem. How an economy performs is the result of many and complex causes. The specific contribution of one of them (such as 'free markets') may be extremely difficult to isolate.

Nevertheless, even a 'casually empiricist' analysis on these lines could perhaps yield *some* helpful clues. We shall return to this point in the concluding chapter of this book.

1.3 Preference, Choice and Self-interest

The case for economic growth, it was argued in section 1.1, rests on enabling preferences or desires of individuals to be fulfilled to a greater extent than before and, in this way, making higher levels of individual welfare possible. In the present section we shall define the concept of preference in a more formal way, take a brief look at the relationship between preference and choice and a longer one at that between preference and self-interest.

Growth is seen by economists as an instrumental good, and economics is concerned in an essential way with problems involved in how to make people better off. Yet such an account may fail to command assent even from some within the ranks of present-day economists themselves. They might readily concede that economists have long been pre-occupied with concerns of this kind but would suggest that this is because economists, like other human beings, are prone to suffer from recurrent attacks of 'value judgement'. Economics itself, they would calim, is a 'positive discipline, not a normative one: the notion of an individual being better off cannot therefore be a basic concept of economics, which can deal only with matters of observable choice. This claim is mistaken. Let us start from the standard and succinct account of the foundations of economic theory provided by Hahn and Hollis. In their introduction they describe foundations of economic theory as follows: 'It is assumed that he (i.e. the economic agent) has preferences and the characterization is by the kind of preferences he has.'[18]

Formally, preference is regarded as a binary relation on the set of outcomes of actions open to the agent, and it assumed to satisfy certain properties such that he can arrange all those outcomes in a complete order. The assumption that the agent knows his possible actions and their consequences and that this behaviour is 'optimizing' entails that he will choose the action leading to his most preferred outcome. With a few more relatively weak assumptions about an agent's preference ordering, it can be numerically represented by a utility function such that his utility from x is higher than that from y if and only if he prefers x to y. Choosing one's most preferred outcome is thus the same as maximizing one's utility function subject to the relevant constraints. If, because of uncertainty, outcomes are not uniquely determined by an agent's actions, the same analysis holds, except that utility is replaced by its mathematical expectation.

We shall now look briefly at the relationship between preference and choice. It has been widely held that the choice that matters in economic theory has nothing to do with preference in the ordinary sense of the word. Ordinarily, a person, to quote from the Oxford English Dictionary, is said to prefer x to y if he has an 'estimation for or liking of' x 'before or above' y; and in a great many contexts such a person may also be regarded as one who thinks he would be better off with x rather than y. Indeed, frequently the statements that a person chooses x rather than y, that he prefers x to y and that he thinks he would be better off with x rather than y are used interchangeably. In *The Importance of Being Earnest*, on being told that he would have to choose between this world, the next world and Australia, Algernon responds by saying that the accounts he had received of Australia and the next world were not particularly encouraging and this world was good enough for him.[19] Algernon, it is clear, interprets choosing something as being better off if he does. On the contrary, so goes the argument, 'preference' or 'utility' as used in modern economic theory and defined above, carry no such 'mentalist' notions; they are simply to be interpreted as other names for observed consistent choice.

'A utility function', asserts a recent textbook of economic theory, 'is a convenient way to describe preferences but it should not be given any psychological interpretation'.[20] The weak Axiom of revealed preference is indeed a requirement of consistency: if in a given situation an individual chooses x when y was possible, in the sense for example of being within his budget, he should not in any situation choose y when x was possible. A person who satisfied this axiom is then said to reveal his preference for x over y. This is *not* as some have thought a tautology, for 'inconsistent' choice could be observed, and since, as Samuelson has shown, the standard results of the theory of consumers' choice follow from the axioms of revealed preference, the theory is said to be, at long last, freed from the ordinary notions of preference and utility. But if choice *is* preference observed, that is it is not *based on* preference, why should choosing x in one particular situation when y is also possible *and* y in another when x is also possible be regarded as inconsistent at all, rather than being simply different? They *appear* to be inconsistent precisely because of a feeling that the two choices cannot reflect the same preference ordering.[21]

In many other contexts as well, interpreting preference only as consistent choice and nothing more simply will not do. The concept of a Pareto-efficient point, i.e. a situation where, given preferences and technology, no one could be made better off without somebody else being worse off is one such context. So are judgements about the consequences of economic growth with which this study is largely concerned. In other words, in a great many contexts where the application of economic theory may be called for, the welfare and the choice aspects of the notion of preference are *both* required for economic analysis to be interesting. Happily much of the recent work in theoretical economics *is* in this direction.

Putting the notion of an individual being better off rather than simply being consistent in the centre of the picture has the important advantage that one need no longer feel obliged to spend so much energy in trying to build a fragile wall between prediction and policy, between a positive and a normative economics. But certain other problems of interpretation remain. The relationship of the concept of preference to that of self-interest becomes particularly difficult to interpret. Standard economic theory usually assumes that the two are identical. But this surely implies too narrow a view of the mainsprings of human action. Are people really motivated in this way? And would it even be rational to be concerned only with self-interest?

The assumption of self-interested preferences itself may be interpreted in a number of different ways. One is to define self-interest in such broad terms that practically anything is covered by it: this has been described as 'definitional egoism'. If someone is observed to help others, sacrificing his own interest for this purpose, this is explained by saying that the person concerned has an interest in helping others: egoism subsumes altruism. On this definition, the statement that preferences are self-interested is trivially true. It has often been supposed that the assumption of utility maximization is tautological in the same way, i.e. that whatever people maximize is called utility. Some textbooks of economics have indeed been guilty of failing to distinguish between a substantive claim which could in principle be disproved by experience and a definitional device. But the distinction has long been recognized, among others by Bentham who wrote (commenting on the 'trite' observation that man is never governed by anything but his own interest): 'This observation, in a large and extensive sense of the word interest (as comprehending all sorts of motives) is indubitably true, but as indubitably false in any of the confined senses in which, upon such an occasion, the word *interest* is wont to be made use of.'[22] It is 'the confined senses' which are relevant.

The semantic view of self-interest has sometimes been confused with the cynical view that people are motivated *only* by their selfish desires: they might on occasion profess to other goals or even behave as if they were guided by them but really this is mere pretence. The cynical view has a long history. A fairly sophisticated version of it was argued by the Legalist school in ancient China in opposition to Confucians who believed in the objective existence of a moral sense in man, both in the sense of right conduct and of a benevolent disposition towards humanity; fortunately for the future of Chinese civilization, the Legalists had the worse of the argument. A somewhat cruder version of the cynical view, presented in Mandeville's *Fable of the Bees*, was summed by by Adam Smith as follows: 'All public spirit, therefore, all preference of public to private interest is, according to him a mere cheat and imposition upon mankind.'[23] It is difficult to take the cynical view seriously. As Smith goes on to observe, 'If an action, supposed to proceed from gratitude, should be discovered to have arisen from an expectation of some new favour, or if what was apprehended to proceed from public spirit, should be found out to have taken its origin from the hope of a pecuniary reward, such a discovery would entirely destroy all notion of merit or praise, worthiness in either of these actions'.[24] Smith does not doubt either that 'discovery' is possible or that such behaviour is not generally the case. Adam Smith's lead was followed by most economists. Cairnes' statement, for example, that 'benevolence and public spirit are extensively influential in human affairs' (even though they cannot at present substitute for the desire for individual advancement and wellbeing),[25] is not untypical of mainstream economists. This is quite contrary to the view that egoism is all.

The cynical view is contrary to experience. Not only is egoism not necessarily characteristic of *all* areas of human behaviour, there are areas where it is generally regarded as uncharacteristic, for example love, friendship and family relationships. Indeed, for such concerns, self-interest as such can hardly provide a rationale, a point which has always been recognized in the common language. A man who 'reject(s) all private friendship, if no interest of self-love intermix itself' observed Hume, . . . abuses terms, and confounds the ideas of things'.[26]

In the case of political behaviour, such as voting, the issue is perhaps less clear-cut, but theories of 'strategic voting', which assume that voters are insincere and egoistic, have provided few clues as to *actual* patterns of voting. Similarly, according to the 'free-riding' hypothesis, benefits derived from a public good cannot be truly revealed by answers to a questionnaire, for any one individual gains by understating his willingness to pay, knowing that this would lead to his having to pay less but would leave total supply (which also equals his individual consumption) unaffected; but there is no strong *empirical* support for the hypothesis itself.[27] Even purely 'private' economic transactions cannot continue to occur regularly in the absence of certain principles of conduct other than self-interest alone.

At a fairly rudimentary level of the development of society, rules requiring a certain degree of honesty and truthfulness in dealings with others are essential for society to function. We might well be justified in doubting if a group without such rules could be described as a society at all. Because so much of common experience flatly contradicts what the cynical interpretation of self-interest asserts, those who do interpret self-interest in this way often seek to provide a rationale of the discrepancy.

One that has been invoked for this purpose is the force of law. An early instance of this position is to be found in Plato's *Republic*, where Glaucon argues that men ' . . . are only diverted into the path of justice by the force of law'.[28] Self-interest on this view is the ruling passion in all human activity, but it is kept in check by legal sanction. But this cannot provide a satisfactory explanation of non-egoistic behaviour. And to say that *this* is what keeps egoism at bay is question-begging, for one can ask what makes such coercion work. Law provides binding rules and rules there must be if society is to develop at all. But the rules themselves could be obeyed from a variety of motives, such as prudential calculation of one's long-run interest; genuine (i.e. non-self-interested) regard for the welfare of others, respect for the rules and so on.

The fear of sanctions may not be the only or even the primary motive for obedience to law but merely a guarantee that those who would voluntarily obey, for example because of their regard for the public good, are not at risk of being sacrificed to those who would not. Such an interpretation of the nature of legal sanctions also fits better with experience, for had egoism in its narrow sense been an all-pervasive motive, violations of the law would surely have far exceeded what they are, even in the most violent of cities, especially where law enforcement agencies are relatively weak.

The cynical view, which remained discredited for a long time, is currently enjoying a new lease of life via the 'selfish gene' argument, derived from the theory of natural selection. Selfish creatures (and human beings in particular) would be able to leave more descendants carrying their genes than would non-selfish creatures. Hence, so runs the argument, only selfish ('rational economic') men would survive. In its more sophisticated versions, the argument can also take care of certain types of altruistic behaviour which are consistent with genetic success. While genetic factors can undoubtedly be of considerable importance in explaining certain aspects of individual human behaviour, the 'selfish gene' argument is a dubious one. A crucial distinction between human beings on the one hand and ants, bees and baboons on the other is the existence in the former case of non-genetic influences, sometimes described as tradition and culture, which affects human social institutions and behaviour; and it is this that explains both the variety of such behaviour and its capacity for change. The stability of the social insects' institutions, as the distinguished biologist Jaques Monod has pointed out, owes next to nothing to cultural heritage, but virtually everything to genetic transmission. Such stability can never be attained by human social institutions.[29]

Since the time-span relevant for genetic change is far longer than that for changes in socio-economic behaviour, genetic explanations of such behaviour have to fall back on some assumption of genetic inertia. Human groups larger than small tribes have existed for, relatively speaking, only a short period. With conventional assumptions about the speed of evolution, the human gene pool could have changed very little in this time. Therefore, if human social behaviour is genetically determined, such behaviour must reflect the conditions of hunter–gatherer life.[30] Hence, so runs the argument, although man's society changed faster than his genes, his behaviour *now* still reflects, through inertia, genetic conditioning acquired at the hunter–gatherer stage. But such a belief amounts to little more than an act of faith. On the genetic interpretation, it is non-egoistic behaviour in any context which required an explanation. Its adherents are constrained to say that any observed human behaviour which appears to be tainted by such characteristics as trust, charity, altruism, public concern or moral commitment and cannot plausibly be regarded as leading to genetic success, is really another instance of egoism in disguise, i.e. to fall back on the semantic interpretation, which we have already dismissed. Alternatively, they must fall back on a claim that such behaviour must *somehow* contribute to genetic success.

Justifying the assumption of egoism by genetic determinism is only apparently 'scientific'. Another leading biologist, Peter Medawar,[31] provides a salutary corrective . . .

We can jettison all reasoning based upon the idea that changes in society happen in the style and under the pressures of ordinary genetic evolution; abandon any idea that the direction of social change is governed by laws other than laws which have at some time been the subject of human decisions or acts of mind. That competition between one man and another is a necessary part of the texture of society; that societies are organisms which grow and must inevitably die; that division of labour within a society is akin to what we can see in colonies of insects; that the laws of genetics have an overriding authority; that social evolution has a direction forcibly imposed upon it by agencies beyond man's control – all these are biological judgments; but, I do assure you, bad judgements based upon a bad biology.

It is this 'bad biology' that underlies much of the work of economists using a biological 'paradigm'.

The traditional argument for the assumption of self-interested behaviour was more pragmatic. This would regard such behaviour neither as the unchanging essence of human nature nor as part of the grand design of evolution but rather as arising from the 'situational logic' of certain kinds of activity and/or certain stages of the development of human society. The importance of the stage of development of society in determining the basis of economic behaviour was particularly stressed by Karl Marx, but a generally pragmatic approach to the status of self-interest is itself pervasive in classical political economy as well as in later economic writing. Wicksell provides a particularly lucid exposition:

We can, for example, safely assume that men are activated by selfish motives, because that is always, at least to a very large extent, true. But we can no more assume that they are filled with a desire to injure each other than that they are purely altruistic. Further, the conditions from which we abstract must be relatively unessential, at least as regards the question under discussion: when we are considering certain economic problems such as, for example, price formation, we may forget that man is not entirely individualistic but has also social impulses. But we must not do so in other problems, as for example in the politico-social field or in the science of public finance.[32]

Even in the areas in which the assumption of selfish motives was applicable, Wicksell thought that it should be regarded only as a first approximation, and that one should try, as economic knowledge developed, to take into consideration more and more of the conditions at first omitted. It is this cautious and limited defence of the assumption of self-interest which has generally been characteristic of economic analysis, and it is clearly far removed from the cynical view of human behaviour which we sketched earlier. Why then do people continue to write that economics is founded on just such a cynical view? One reason could be a misreading of the text. Some well-known passages by economists that are often quoted as showing that economics is based on a fundamentalist interpretation of the self-interest assumption in fact show no such thing. We shall cite two examples of this. The first occurs in Adam Smith's *Wealth of Nations*:

Man has almost constant occasion for the help of his bretheren It is in vain for him to expect it from their benevolence only . . . It is not from the benevolence from the butcher, the brewer or the baker that we expect our dinner, but from their regard for their own interest. . . . We address ourselves, not to their humanity but to their self-love, and never talk to them of our own necessities but of their advantages.[33]

In saying this, Smith was not asserting that self-interested behaviour was all pervasive but precisely the opposite, for we expect much more than our dinner. To say that benevolence is not the only motive influencing human behaviour is not the same as saying that self-interest *is*.

A second statement, which is frequently quoted as showing that economists do accept the cynical view of human nature, is due to Edgeworth: 'The first principle of economics is that every agent is activated only by self-interest.'[34] Indeed the statement seems plain enough until one notices Edgeworth's footnote qualifying this remark, namely that this is a 'description rather' (i.e. description rather than principle) but a description 'sufficient for the purpose of these tentative studies', which suggests that Edgeworth intended the description as a heuristic device for an analysis of a limited aspect of human behaviour rather than as a fundamental principle with universal applicability. That this is indeed the correct interpretation of Edgeworth's famous statement is confirmed by his subsequent statement on the same page of *Mathematical Psychics*, on which the first occurs: 'Between the two extremes, Pure Egoistic and Pure Universalistic, there may be an infinite number of impure methods; wherein the happiness of others as compared by the agent (in a calm moment) with his own neither counts for nothing not yet counts for one but counts for a fraction.'

Such statements, and I could quote many more, suggest that mainstream economics took a much more cautious and complex view of the role of egoism in human behaviour than is generally supposed. That the point continues to be missed by critics reflects careless reading on their part,[35] though economists themselves are not without blame for this state of affairs; they have not always distinguished clearly enough between a heuristic assumption and a universal truth, and between a prima facie principle (which may have to contend with others) and an over-riding one (which by definition dominates all others).

Our argument above has been that self-interest, in economics, is rightly interpreted as a prima facie principle which neither excludes nor necessarily or always dominates other principles.[36] It is only if self-interest excludes all considerations of others' interest or if it rides roughshod over them, that it can be regarded as equivalent to selfishness. Traditional economic theory assigns self-interest an important role but by no means the only role in the play. The view of economic man as a narrowminded 'rational fool' is largely a caricature, and caricatures can be useful only if they are recognized as such. Yet, taking the complexity of human behaviour into account does not by itself help find a proper basis for the concept of preference. The critics of economic theory have after all been addressing a genuine question, namely, *is* there a common standard of 'preference' in terms of which the different kinds of objectives that appear to be appropriate in different contexts could themselves be judged? The question has long been discussed under the rubric of the relationship between 'economic' and 'non-economic' aspects of welfare. This relationship is discussed briefly in the next section.

1.4 Welfare: Economic and Non-economic Aspects

One solution to the problem just noted was first clearly formulated by Graaff and has now become almost a part of the received doctrine; non-economic variables *do* affect welfare but they are to be thought of as exogenous in the sense that they influence economic variables without being influenced by them.[37]

As long as there is such a one-way causal relationship, the analysis of welfare in terms of economic variables remains valid. It may be questioned whether the solution is satisfactory. An assumption, for example, that even though the state of the environment might affect welfare it is not itself affected by, say, the volume of aluminium production, would be to assume away the problem itself. In much recent debate on the limits of growth, it is the effect of economic variables on others which have not traditionally been considered by economists, that lies at the heart of the matter. Other solutions are possible. One may grant for example, that economic variables influence non-economic ones but go on to make some judgement about the nature or direction of that influence. This has, in fact, been the usual approach of economists, who have assumed further, that their influence is benign. For instance, a recurrent theme in classical political economy is the non-economic dimensions of urban housing. There are whole districts in contemporary England, observes Senior, in which a working-class family occupies not one room but one corner of a room; and those who live in cellars are a step even lower in wretchedness.[38] Such habitation is damp, lets in neither light nor air and is invariably situated in the immediate neighbourhood of uncovered sewers from which filth is seldom removed. Mere residence in such places, Senior points out, is enough to produce illness and disease, which must inevitably spread rapidly through contagion. It is impossible, he observes, that a population lodged in such a manner should be in a good condition either physically or morally. Indeed, housing is such an important component of the standard of living *because* many 'non-economic' aspects of life are adversely affected by poor housing. In all classes of society, states Senior, but particularly in the lower, many of the domestic virtues depend mainly on a comfortable home. 'Where that does not exist, the husband and father is almost irresistibly impelled to seek his pleasures abroad and gradually acquires habits under which the earnings, that ought to have clothed and educated and perhaps even fed his wife and children, are wasted by the fireside of the public house.'[39]

At a more general level, it is the non-economic effects of poverty that is the opening theme of Alfred Marshall's *Principles of Economics*, but his emphasis was not so much on the attainment of virtue, nor for that matter on happiness, but on human dignity. What troubled him most was the deadening of the higher faculties that conditions surrounding extreme poverty tend to produce. Marshall saw clearly that in the England of his time there was a hard core of the urban poor who had little opportunity for friendship, who knew nothing of the decencies and the quiet and very little of the unity of family life and whom religion often failed to reach.[40] While their physical, mental and moral ill-health could be due in part to other causes as well, poverty was clearly 'the chief cause'.[41] In addition to this hard core ('. . . the Residuum of our large towns') there are, Marshall wrote:

. . . numbers of people both in town and country who are brought up with insufficient food, clothing and house-room, whose education is broken off early in order that they may go to work for wages, who henceforth are engaged during long hours in exhausting toil with imperfectly nourished bodies and have therefore no chance of developing their higher mental faculties.[42]

Poverty led to stunted and degraded lives. The study of the causes of poverty was therefore ipso facto 'a study of the causes of degradation of a large part of mankind'.[43] The time had come, he thought, to question why such degradation should exist at all, 'whether it was really impossible that all should start the world with a fair chance of leading a cultured life, free from the pains of poverty and the stagnating influences of excessive mechanical toil'.[44]

That economic growth would promote rather than hinder non-economic welfare in countries where per capita income is low, continues to be believed by most economists, although doubts have been expressed on whether this is any longer true of developed countries. However, a specific a priori judgement of this nature is not really necessary for the approach itself to be valid. All that is required is that one no longer regards 'other' sources of welfare as necessarily constant, with regard to economic variables proper, but tries to reason directly on the basis of relevant evidence how they are likely to be affected by changes in economic conditions.

Though many practical difficulties arise in reaching an over-all judgement in any particular case, in some instances, such as environmental pollution, considerable progress has in fact been made towards formulating comprehensive methods of cost–benefit calculations, which can take such effects into account.[45] But there are others where the conceptual difficulties involved appear to be of a more fundamental kind. Welfare arising from personal relationships belongs to this category. The problem is essentially one of comparability. In the standard theory, preference orderings are assumed to be 'connected'; given any two feasible alternatives, x and y, the weak preference relation R is such that at least one of the statements xRy and yRx must hold for every individual. This ensures comparability among alternatives. If the relevant alternatives include 'economic' as well as 'non-economic' components, the assumption of connectedness is especially difficult to justify. This may explain why people often feel uncomfortable about the use of economic theory when the alternatives over which preferences are defined are extended indefinitely.

In a perceptive discussion of this problem Wolff[46] notes 'the incongruity of applying a terminology drawn from one field to phenomena usually considered in an entirely different field' and points out that things such as religion, family life or personal relationships are not necessarily capable of being treated in terms of the same model as economic transactions. For this reason, he finds the use of indifference curve analysis to pronounce on such questions 'creepy' and even inhuman. I have considerable sympathy for Wolff's position, but would like to add the following riders. First, the point at issue here is quite distinct from the question, considered earlier, about non-economic consequences of economic growth. Economists, it may be recalled, had been much concerned with the deadening effects on family life of poverty and squalor, which led them to hope that economic growth would help improve the quality of life in this respect. The point being considered here is whether levels (and changes in levels) of economic wellbeing and non-economic elements of wellbeing (however these are brought about) are directly comparable. Secondly, even if *full* comparability of welfare as between economic and non-economic alternatives does not hold, a less demanding 'kind' of comparability could be postulated. Little progress in this direction has been achieved as yet.[47]

2
The Determination of Individual Preferences

La croyance au sens de la vie suppose toujours une échelle de
valeurs, un choix, nos préférences.
Albert Camus, *Le Mythe de sisyphe*

A charge against economics that I have discussed at some length
is that of regarding self-interest as the only motive of human
action. Many fellow social scientists believe such a tendency to
be itself the result of a more basic failing of the economist, his
narrow and blinkered vision. This failing, they say, persists only
because of the economist's studied lack of curiosity about the
origin of preference orderings. The economist takes individual
preference orderings as given. Despite the central role they play
in economic theory, he does not proceed further to enquire how
preferences come to be what they are. In particular, economists
are chided for neglecting to take *social* influences on human
behaviour into account. An instance of such a complaint by a
distinguished sociologist was cited earlier, in the first section of
chapter 1.

Marxist scholars have emphasized that economic behaviour is
by definition *social* behaviour and hence that an analysis of
individual economic behaviour in isolation from the social
relations of production is not merely false but even meaningless.
More recently some philosophically minded economic theorists
have derided the standard notion of optimization by an economic
agent as simplistic, even feeble-minded.[1] The social origins of
individual preferences, they argue, must be made an explicit part
of the analysis for economic theory to be either useful or
interesting. Some of the more important issues that arise in this
context are briefly discussed in this chapter, which consists of
three sections. The first section examines in what sense if any,

individual preferences can be said to be socially influenced or determined, and corresponding implications for the concept and measurement of social wellbeing. Section 2.2 criticizes some doctrines of socio-cultural determinism as applied to the Third World. The last section considers some possible effects of economic growth on culture.

2.1 Individual preference: The Social Dimension

That individual preferences have a social dimension seems, on the face of it, to be an eminently reasonable proposition. Few, I imagine, would be disposed to argue to the contrary. Some doctrinaire advocates of genetic determinism might, of course, believe that preferences are innate and given at birth, that for instance every little boy or girl who comes into this world alive is either a little liberal or else a conservative, and that whether one would rather have turnip than spinach or the other way round, could be given in just the same way right from the beginning. However, I have already stated my reasons for rejecting genetic explanations of economic behaviour. But preferences must come from somewhere. It is plausible that they come from society. However, people who assert the social origins of individual preferences often have quite different things in mind. The statement that individual preferences have a social origin may simply be a more dramatic way of saying that the exercise of such preferences can only occur in a social context. If so, such a statement is likely to carry with it a further implication, namely an individual's preference ordering of a given set of alternatives may vary depending on the particular social context in which it is exercised.

The same point is sometimes made, though with a certain change of emphasis, by saying that an individual has different roles to play and his preferences vary with the role he plays. To take a familiar example, a producer of wheat may be in favour of policies that have the effect of raising its price, while a consumer of wheat would normally prefer policies that tend to lower this price; but the same individual could be both a consumer and a producer of wheat. A jogger is likely to have a different preference ordering with regard to a set of alternative schemes of traffic regulation, as compared to a motorist but the same individual could be jogging or driving depending on the time of day; and so on. For the purpose of social evaluation, preference orderings of an individual in different roles could be considered simply as different preference orderings, to be taken into account in the total reckoning. Alternatively, each individual's preference in his role as a citizen may be regarded as the only relevant preferences.

Clearly, the precise context in which a preference relation on alternatives is postulated can be extremely important and more attention to it would greatly help clarity of thought. Hence, to rule out societal facts, per se, as inadmissible evidence for the purpose of choice theory because they do not directly provide information regarding individual preference or utility is surely quite mistaken. Yet this is standard practice in economics. However, this can be rectified without abandoning the standard tools of economic theory itself. All that is required is to play close attention to the context in which the preferences in question are to be exercised. No great *analytical* difficulties for the theory of preference appear to arise on this score.

Another aspect of the influence of social considerations on behaviour, one which has been much discussed by social anthropologists, is the constraints that they tend to impose on an individual's choice. Social conventions often have the effect of pre-empting particular commodity combinations, or more generally, particular states of nature from being chosen. Taboos, by definition, are examples of such restriction. Whether they arise from custom, fashion, religion or tribal lore, their effect is to rule out, for those who adhere to them, certain items of consumption, e.g. of food and drink (beef, pork, meat on particular days of the week or year or for particular groups of people, meat at any time, red meat with white wine etc) or of clothing (with a wide range of variation from one society to another as to which parts of the body must be kept covered, or even possibly of which must not be) and certain kinds of behaviour. Social conventions may also be of the prescribing rather than the prohibiting kind, taking the form as it were, of totem rather than taboo. Certain choices or certain ways of behaviour may win friends or confer status. Mores can make things right, i.e. give rise to norms. Moral judgements can be imbibed from one's social milieu. All these could influence individual's preferences.

How wide the range of behaviour to which such conventions (whether positive or negative) apply, how detailed and categorical the instructions they give, and how closely people's actual behaviour conforms to them in letter and spirit, have varied greatly between different societies. If, in fact, they are wide in scope, detailed in specification and effective in regulating conduct, the constraints they impose on individual choice may well in effect determine individual choice entirely, in the sense that 'free' choices (those not determined by social convention) could constitute a 'null set'. This seems unlikely, but in societies which prescribe and enforce elaborate codes of conduct, spelling out in the minutest detail what members of each status or caste group may or may not do, it is not perhaps such a bad description of reality. The degree of specificity of social conventions and the closeness of fit between these and actual choices may both be used as measures of the degree of traditionalism of a society.

That in all societies irrespective of whether they are modern or traditional, individual preferences and choice behaviour are strictly determined by social conditioning is precisely the contention of an influential school of thought, which has been variously described as collectivism, holism or institutionalism. This is an element which in some form or other is common to doctrines that, in other respects, differ greatly from one another, such as those associated with the names of Hegel, Marx and Burke. The view described is pervasive in the writings of mainstream sociologists; for this reason Pettit, with only mild exaggeration, has described the sociologist's picture of man as 'a cultural dope, an ideological dolt and a rule-bound dimwit'.[2] In recent years the 'social-determinist' view of individual choice has been developed in a particularly systematic and thorough-going way by a group of behaviourist psychologists led by B. F. Skinner. It is this version of determinism on which I shall concentrate in the following exposition. In Skinner's view, individual behaviour is fully determined by the social environment. This environment is conceived in very broad terms.

Sometimes, Skinner calls it 'culture', the culture into which an individual is born, being 'composed of all the variables affecting him which is arranged by other people'.[3] Since one's genetic endowment is certainly 'arranged by other people' it should by this definition be reckoned to be part of the total social environment or culture that determines behaviour. (Strictly interpreted, Skinner's definition of culture thus differs from the one usual in the literature of sociology, namely as the totality of *non-genetic* determinants of learned behaviour, but in practice the thrust of his discussion is not very different.) Culture also has a historical component, for the environment includes its own past.

What distinguishes Skinner's from other brands of determinism however, is not that it takes account of the past (they all do) but its over-riding concern with the present and immediate environment and in that environment with the 'contingencies of reinforcement'. These are events or consequences that are arranged by the society contingent on various types of behaviour by the individual. If the behaviour is of a kind approved of or desired by the society or culture in which it occurs, positive reinforcers follow: if it is not, negative or 'aversive' reinforcers are the result. Contingencies of reinforcement can take different forms in different societies of human beings or of animals. It is the proper arrangement of such contingencies that constitutes the essential task of a society and it is these that make men, or mice, tick. In some societies the business of reinforcement is carried out principally by the government, in others a wide variety of agencies are involved. But the effect is the same, namely not only control of individual behaviour but control of it even in areas of choice where individuals are apparently free to make their own decisions, subject only to the constraints imposed by income. In contemporary American society, for instance, according to Skinner, if individuals wear particular kinds of clothing, go to particular movies or observe a particular pattern of sexual behaviour, it is only because of the control exercised by family, friends, education, religion, work and so on. Hence the approach itself is said to be based on the 'operant conditioning paradigm'. Clearly it is far removed from the paradigm of the optimizing individual, which underlies economic theory, even though the optimization is subject to constraints in economic theory as well.

A recent, and not unsympathetic, review of Skinner's approach to behavioural therapy sums up this approach as follows:

In the Skinnerian orientation, the culture, through parents, peers and others socializing agents shapes the individual by reinforcing the behaviour it desires and punishing behaviour it does not desire, conditioning anxiety reactions to some situations and not to others, teaching norms of acceptable behaviour, shaping the person's standards of art and morality and so forth.[4]

Not all economists who assert that individual preferences are socially determined would go as far as Skinner. Many would be inclined to reject some at least of his conclusions as fundamentally anti-humanist, and would probably wish to describe only some, not *all*, human desires as socially determined. Yet Skinner's work is valuable precisely because it works out in full the logic of a certain position, one which seeks to explain individual behaviour by causes rather than reasons.

What difference then, if any, does taking social influences into account make to the economic analysis of individual behaviour? To answer this question properly we must return to the inter-relationship between preference, choice and welfare which was described earlier. The interpretative significance of economic theory, it was argued, rests on this inter-relationship. The statement xPy for a given individual and two given alternatives, x and y, is at once a statement about his preference ordering (x comes above y in this ordering), his choice (he will choose x if he can) and his welfare (he will be better off with/at x, than y). But complications can arise. The conceptual link between an individual's preference and his choice is subject to the limitation that what he can choose is constrained by his income. This, indeed, is what the theory of revealed preference focuses on. The alternatives x and y in that theory are naturally interpreted as alternative commidity combinations. If an individual is observed to choose x but we know also that given his income and the prices concerned, y was beyond his reach, we cannot then state that xPy. In fact, in such a case, *no* inference about the underlying preference ordering or about his relative welfare levels can be made from his choice alone.

A similar argument, namely that a person cannot be said to express a preference for something that he chooses when prevented by force or compulsion from choosing an alternative, has been used to settle the question whether migration from rural areas to factory towns during the Industrial Revolution in England can be construed as evidence for a rise in the standard of living. Thus, according to some historians, if migration was mainly induced by enclosures that forced people off the land, it cannot be so construed; but, if as much recent work suggests, there was little direct compulsion, it can.[5]

The same principle is involved in the case we are considering now, where constraints on individual choice arise from social conventions rather than from income or from force. If social conventions beyond the individual's control constrain his decisions, one could argue that his preferences, hence levels of welfare, cannot logically be inferred from his behaviour. John Stuart Mill states this more succinctly: 'He, who does anything because it is the custom makes no choice.'[6] Indeed one could go further. If the constraints imposed by social conventions are non-trivial, in the sense that they lead to patterns of behaviour that are in some way different from those that would have come about if such conventions were not there, there must be some individuals for which in some pairwise comparison the chosen alternative is the one that was *not* preferred.

The view that individual desires are completely determined by social forces rather than merely constrained by them, gives rise to even greater difficulties of interpretation. It could be argued that it is what in any given context, preferences are, not how they came to be what they are, that matters. The point is formally similar to that stated earlier (chapter 1, section 1.4) when considering the relationship between economic and non-economic variables affecting an individual choice. It was observed that provided it was non-economic variables that determined economic factors and not the other way around, no conceptual difficulty need arise. Should not the same be true of the relationship between individual preferences and society? If it is society that determines individual preferences while the effect of individual preferences on society can be neglected, why should the results of choice theory be affected at all?

Contrariwise, it may be held that if one's preferences are to be regarded as being entirely conditioned by one's society and culture, there is little point in continuing to regard the satisfaction of such preferences as the primary source of one's wellbeing. Indeed if they *are* so conditioned, we may even ask whether it is useful to speak of *individual* preferences at all, let alone their bearing on welfare. We may think that it would be more useful to concentrate on the *process* of conditioning rather than its product. And this is precisely what Skinner and his followers attempt to do. Conceptually, links between the economist's traditional notions of preference and utility on the one hand and 'contingencies of reinforcement' on the other are not, it is true, particularly difficult to establish. Skinner himself notes in passing: 'When our behaviour is positively reinforced, we say we enjoy what we are doing; we call ourselves happy'.[7] But this is not a line of thought that he actually pursues anywhere in his work. This is essentially because the philosophies underlying the two approaches, their visions of what the world is like, are quite different. Concepts of individual choice or individuals' responsibility for their actions can never provide a proper basis for an analysis of 'efficient reinforcing contingencies' because they carry 'a semantic cargo of a quite different sort'.[8] This cargo is both unnecessary and burdensome.

Concepts of choices based on individual preference inevitably rely on mentalistic notions, which according to tenets of behaviouristic philosophy have no scientific interest or validity. And to the extent that individual preference, feelings, desires and so on exist at all, they are themselves *products* of the environment. 'What we feel when we have feelings and what we observe through introspection are nothing more than a rather miscellaneous set of collateral products or byproducts of the environmental conditions to which behaviour is related.'[9] Hence, trying to explain choice by preference is a futile task. 'We do not act because we feel like acting, for example, we act and feel like acting for a common reason . . . '[10] namely the environmental conditions, the contingencies of reinforcement in particular. It is therefore ' . . . only by turning from man *qua* man to the external conditions of which his behaviour is a function'[11] that the understanding of behaviour and the design of efficient techniques of control are possible. From this point of view it is right and proper to avoid talking about an individual's wants, norms, desires, needs and so on. Reinforcement, conditioning, counter-conditioning, extinction and so on are the appropriate concepts.

A rejection of individual preferences does not necessarily imply a rejection of the concept of social wellbeing itself. As the comment quoted above (on p. 33) brings out, this approach imputes desires to entities such as society or culture rather than to individuals. The level of wellbeing of a society will depend on the extent to which things are what the culture desires. In principle, therefore, an evaluation of alternative social or institutional arrangements or of states of affairs generally could be carried out from a non-individualistic point of view as well. How it can actually be known what a culture's desires are, is a question on which theories of this sort tend to be somewhat vague. One could, however, think of several different kinds of information from which they could be derived. The current behaviour of the majority of the people in the society concerned may, for instance, be taken as a surrogate, in which case, the greater the size of the minority, the worse off a society would be deemed to be. The 'best practice' as shown by the behaviour of an elite could be used instead.

Society's preferences may be identified with traditional practice or found in an authoritative text, whether this is a religious scripture or its modern secular counterpart. If, as will invariably be the case, the text is ambiguous, or alternatives not covered by it arise, there could be 'proper' authorities empowered to settle points at issue and enforce obedience. The preferences of a government as revealed by its decisions could be accepted as social preferences.[12] And so on. In theory, an 'institutionalist' might have his own evaluation of alternative institutional arrangements, but his point of view will tend to be not the interests of individuals, but the smoothness of the society's operations, the consistency of the operations with traditional patterns or whatever.[13] All these could be interpreted as variants of a concept of the social welfare function described by Bergson, namely that social welfare be regarded as a function, the value of which is understood to depend on all the variables that might be considered as affecting welfare. Clearly, this is a very broad concept, perhaps *too* broad. As Sen has pertinently observed, the decisions on ends which such a function represents could be determined by 'The dictates of an oligarchy or the whims of a dictator or the values of a class or even be given simply by tradition'.[14] But in order to be acceptable, such decisions must have a *moral* justification. A society where behaviour patterns are perfectly in accordance with old traditions and which operates smoothly, with no questions asked, might well, on the view described, be regarded as a society with a high level of social wellbeing, even if the tradition in question is cruel and authoritarian and the smoothness of operation simply due to long practice in exercising it.

Whatever the degree of importance one wishes to give to individual preferences in assessing levels of social wellbeing, to suppose that 'anything goes' would be quite irresponsible. Moral justification for criteria of evaluation of social states is clearly called for. Some ways in which such a justification may be sought are discussed in our next chapter. Meanwhile it is worth noting that the 'social-determinist' view just described, is in a sense a throw-back to the past. It is based on a way of looking at the world which would allow a society to be regarded as flourishing even if the masses of its members were not flourishing at all. The point about economics, I have argued earlier, is precisely that this is *not* allowed. That the traditional view has now been largely discredited is itself in part, the achievement of economics. To go back to it, under the garb of giving the social aspect of individual preferences its due, would be retrograde and futile. Social institutions are indeed important but their purpose is to serve the interest of individuals.

Arguments about the relationship of individual preferences to the prevailing culture need not be quite so starkly opposed as their protagonists have usually made them out to be. One could, after all, believe that individual preferences are deeply influenced by society and culture, but not determined by them. Consider, for instance, the following statement by Lukes[15] on the difference between the sociologist's and the economist's view on individual preferences.

A sociological perspective differs from the individualist picture in revealing all the manifold ways in which individuals are dependent on, indeed *constituted by* the operation of social forces, by all the agencies of socialization and social control, by ecological, institutional and cultural factors, by influences ranging from the primary family group to the value system of the society as a whole. All these views dispute as both naive and mistaken the individualist picture of the individuals forming society as 'independent centres of consciousness', as by nature rational and free, as the sole generators of their own wants and preferences. Their consciousness is rather seen as (partially or wholly) socially determined and their wants and preferences socially patterned.

The rhetoric of the first part of this passage seems to be at odds with its rather tepid conclusion. To say that something is *partly* socially determined is, after all, the same as saying that it is partly *not* so determined; and to claim that wants and preferences are socially *patterned* is quite consistent with believing individual preferences to have a considerable measure of independence, for, conceivably, individuals could weave their own patterns, choosing between a variety of feasible designs. Fuller fledged doctrines of determinism, whether of the social or the biological kind must on the other hand imply that the individual himself plays a completely passive role. This is what makes such doctrines ultimately self-defeating, for the role of the individual in determining his preferences cannot be so whittled down without giving up the notion of individual preference altogether. It is perfectly true that a concept of individual preferences based on desires and not just conditioned by society must let 'mentalist' notions in. Noting this, Skinner himself has complained that our language is replete with mentalism of this kind.[16] This does not constitute a defect of the language, but rather a warning that the concept of individual desires cannot be dispensed with.

At the other end of the spectrum, it has been held by some 'reductionist' advocates of methodological individualism that groups or institutions are 'really' nothing but individuals, that they have no meaning over and beyond the people belonging to them and hence that any talk of 'society' influencing individual preferences can only be so much idle chatter of a transcendental kind! I believe this position, as well, to be quite untenable.[17] A more reasonable approach would be that *both* society at large and the individual himself have an active role to play in determining his preferences. Such an approach would focus on the possibilities of interaction between the individual and society.[18] The relevant point here is that society is not a seamless web. There is no one unique group called 'society' that serves as a reference group for the individuals' preferences. Any one person belongs to many different groups, defined by attributes such as income, occupation, gender, age, class, caste, status, race, language, nationality, political views and so on. Some groups will be regarded by the individual as more important than others, depending on the activity concerned, and on the individual. Even if an individual's preferences are only a reflection of the Joneses', there usually is a choice of *which* Joneses to keep up with, and typically, different Joneses will be chosen in different aspects of his behaviour.[19]

Secondly, even the behaviour of a specific reference group to be emulated tends to be defined in terms of broad categories. They refer to 'characteristics' such that a characteristic can be attained by different possible combinations of items among which an individual must choose.

Thirdly, social norms also change. Theories based on social determinism cannot easily explain the occurrence of such change. Interaction provides a more natural interpretation. Social values and norms, beliefs and behaviour are indeed part of the individual's non-genetic inheritance. But he also observes, reflects, asks questions about his inheritance, learns from himself and from others in his *and* other societies, accepts, rejects or modifies prevailing judgements (including his own) and so on. By doing so, individuals and groups of individuals may under certain circumstances succeed in changing social norms and traditions and in the process their own individual preference orderings might change as well. Once such changes have become effective they may be indistinguishable from the rest of the 'cultural heritage'. This helps explain the phenomenon which Eric Hobsbawm has described as the invention of tradition: 'Traditions which appear or claim to be old are often quite recent in origin and sometimes invented.'[20]

Recently, some economists have drawn attention to the possibility of an individual's utility level changing even without a change occurring in the alternatives chosen or his preference ordering over them. This could be due to a change in his efficiency as a pleasure machine so that he gets more (or less) out of things than before.[21] Changes of this kind could be due simply to a change of mood. If an individual is 'feeling blue', his efficiency as a pleasure machine will be impaired. If he is 'feeling high', it will be increased. But changes brought about in this way can only be temporary. Changes of a more permanent nature could ensue as a result of an individual undergoing a deeply traumatic experience. But this would still affect only the individual concerned. If the effect in question is both long-lasting and widespread, a more broad-based, 'macro' kind of explanation is called for. Revolutionary political change that signals the end of an oppressive regime and promises hope for the many, could be one such explanation ('Bliss it was in that dawn to be alive'). So would gradual processes such as those of scientific discovery and technological progress leading to a fundamental change in the way that people look at the world. But whatever its source, such a process, again, necessarily involves an interaction between individuals and society.

Individual perceptions are affected by social change. But for utility levels and hence the standard of living to rise, social change in turn must be responsive to individual wants and needs. This must also be our conclusion in the case where individual choices and even their preference orderings *are* altered in the process of social change. If the changes concerned reflect a genuine process of learning, if they are associated with a tendency for society to become less repressive and fanatical, more likely to help the individual find his bearings without him being stifled in the process, they could represent an increase in individual utilities and hence in social welfare, no less important than a measured increase in GNP. The changes experienced by societies in the process of industrialization are often of this kind. The more repressive the society, the greater the hazards in inferring preferences from actual choices, including choices from which GNP is computed.

2.2 Socio-cultural Determinism and the Possibility of Development

I have been discussing the implications of socio-cultural determinism for the concept of preference. But, clearly, it also has adverse implications for concepts of progress or development. A central concern of this book is the question of what constitutes economic development. If however, as determinism of this kind implies, desires and attitudes in a traditional culture cannot reflect anything other than the tradition itself, it is doubtful if economic development in any meaningful sense is possible at all. The hopes for removal of mass poverty through economic development so eloquently expressed by the founding fathers of economics must then be dismissed as dangerous delusions. I shall digress briefly from the main theme of this chapter to consider this aspect of the doctrine of cultural determinism in the specific context of the less developed countries.

In the literature of development economics, there has long been a tradition which insists on the primacy of the cultural constraint. Because of such a constraint, so runs the argument, the outward shift of production possibility curves in developing countries through the use of new technology may fail to be achieved, even if an appropriate technology is available. In writings by authors of this school, the undoubted fact that modern industrial civilization first developed among nations of European origin is usually taken as the starting point. This fact is regarded in some way as showing that people other than those of European origin suffer some fundamental lack, which would make the achievement of industrialization especially difficult. This theme of cultural backwardness as the cause of underdevelopment has been propounded with particular zeal by historians and sociologists. Typical of historians who hold this view is Hartwell, who emphasizes 'that the underdeveloped countries of today are the inheritors of civilisations quite different from and quite independent of European civilisations'.[22] Yet, argues Hartwell, it was in Europe since early medieval days that there has been economic growth which was not experienced elsewhere in the world.

It is European civilization long in the making which has provided the matrix of modern economic growth. Indeed, all successfully developed countries in the modern world, except Japan, are either parts of Europe or European societies elsewhere in the world. This does not mean that growth in under-developed countries, comparable with that in Europe is impossible, only that it *may* be impossible and that in any case it will certainly be mnore difficult.[23]

Many social anthropologists have expressed a similar view, though their emphasis is usually slightly different. In contrasting developing with developed countries, what they point to are basic differences in personal characteristics and patterns of behaviour between the peoples concerned, rather than, as is the case with historians, simply the historical experience of the past. This argument was very clearly presented by Boeke[24] in his influential study of 'dualistic' society in pre-independence Indonesia, but the argument itself is intended to be quite general. The crux of the argument is that certain fundamental differences exist between 'Eastern' and 'Western' societies and peoples. Western society according to Boeke is characterized by common sense and reason, Eastern society by fatalism and resignation. Easterners, says Boeke, suffer from a lack of business qualities, organizing power and discipline. In consequence their industrial products fail to come up to 'even the minimum requirements of standard . . . '.[25] Nothing can be done to remedy this lack, because it is not possible to transform the operating forces into the opposite of what they are. The contrast is all-inclusive, it goes too deep. Hence, there is no question of the Eastern producer adapting himself to the Western example technological-ly, economically or socially.[26] Even in cases where the two are concerned in the production of the same commodity, Eastern business will always be quite different from Western. The prospects of economic development in 'Eastern' countries are therefore bleak indeed.

We argue elsewhere in this book that such prophecies of gloom have been falsified. The actual record of economic progress in developing countries since the 1960s has not been unmixed. It varied enormously between different countries and there have been major disasters, especially in parts of Africa.

Nevertheless, industrialization has spread, rates of economic growth in many of the developing countries (including Boeke's Indonesia) have been high and in some instances higher than those attained by any European country over a similar period in the past and a great many people in developing countries have achieved a genuine increase in the standard of living. Therefore, as judged by their ability to make successful predictions, theories based on cultural determinism cannot be said to have performed particularly well. But the problems of their acceptability at a logical level are even more serious, and we shall now proceed to comment briefly on these.

The basic logical problem in theories of this type is how to provide an adequate analytical justification for projecting indefinitely into the past and into the future what are believed to be actual differences between societies or cultures at the present time. For instance, even if Boeke has correctly described differences between 'East' and 'West', his conclusions do not follow unless the differences are shown to be permanent and immutable, and he does not provide any real argument *why* they should be of this kind. However, approaches such as Boeke's become a little more intelligible if they are regarded as based not only on cultural considerations, but on genetic ones *as well*.

As we observed while commenting on Skinner's definition of culture, culture-based explanations of under-development need not necessarily be regarded as alternatives to those based on genetics; the two types of explanation can be complementary. That the stability of the human gene pool, as contrasted with the known record of considerable variability in economic achievement, constitutes a powerful logical objection to a genetic explanation of socio-economic behaviour has already been pointed out. Those who favour such an explanation have sought to answer the objection in a number of ways, a suitably watered down version of the postulate of a master race being especially popular. Some versions of cultural determinism – Boeke's is a clear enough instance – fit quite well into such a conceptual scheme. This is not especially surprising, for culture itself is conceived of by many writers of this school in terms of racial identity. Now, if all human progress could be attributed to the efforts of a particular human group which has the special and enduring advantage of a superior cultural and genetic endowment, with (in some versions) a congenial climate serving as added help, a cultural-cum-racist reading could perhaps be taken to provide if not a compelling, at least an internally consistent, interpretation of the history of civilization. Differences in levels of development among different countries at a given time could then be explained by the 'natural' failure of inferior peoples to measure up to the standards of the 'herrenvolk', while overall economic and technological advance over time could be taken as reflecting the continuing improvement in the cultural heritage of the latter.

Unfortunately for such a 'synthesis', and no less unfortunately for the Hartwell thesis, the historical record shows quite clearly that neither technical nor economic progress has been the preserve of any particular culture, society, ethnic group or civilization. As Tawney once remarked, history with its record of the movement of leadership from region to region, 'lends little support to the theory that certain peoples are naturally qualified for success in the economic arts, and others unfitted for it'.[27] Hartwell's or Boeke's theory of course, amounts to just that and there are many others who share this opinion. Indeed, the view that people of European origin are naturally qualified for success in the economic (and other) arts in a way that others are not, has become so much a part of received doctrine that even scholars, whose discipline trains them to be highly sceptical, tend to accept it unquestioningly. This cannot be attributed simply to the fact that Europeans *have* been highly successful in the economic arts. So after all have the Japanese, and of late, those from Korea, Singapore and elsewhere. Presumably, the difference is that Europeans were pioneers and leaders of industrial civilization, whereas the Japanese were merely followers. But, the point that Tawney was trying to make was precisely this: different peoples have led economic and technical progress at different times. This is quite missed out by the cultural determinists, who have confined their attention to the relatively recent past.

The Industrial Revolution does, no doubt, mark a decisive advance in human development. But so, in its time, did the discovery of agriculture. The domestication of animals and the cultivation of food plants were, in all probability, first developed in the Near East. Further, the transmission of agricultural economies into a Europe which had previously been populated only with hunting and food-gathering communities appears to a quite considerable extent to have been the result of imported technology.[28] The 'ultimately Oriental origin' of most of the principal elements in European Neolithic cultures is stated by Clark and Piggot[29] to be 'a recognized commonplace'. Nor did the most important innovations of the next period, namely the discovery of writing and the organization or urban life, first occur in Europe.

Civilized, i.e. literate, urban and politically integrated communities first appeared in Europe much later than on the Nile, the Euphrates or in the Indus Valley and very little earlier than in North China.[30] The predominantly East–West direction of the movement of technology was not limited to pre-historic times alone, but was also characteristic of some later periods, especially after the decline of Rome. In describing the developments in technology during the millennium 500 to 1500, Singer observes:

For nearly all branches of technology the best products available to the West were those of the Near East, at first those from the Byzantine Empire and later also from the Islamic Caliphate or from Persia. . . . It was largely by imitation and in the end sometimes by improvement of the techniques and models that had come from or through the Near East that the products of the West ultimately rose to excellence . . . .[31]

The considerable Chinese contribution to the development of technology is also now well-known.[32]

Yet, it was by people belonging to a region that had long been relatively backward that the next decisive step in human advance was achieved. Such an event is itself quite contrary to what doctrines of genetic–cultural determinism would predict, a point recently noted by Gellner:

The regions of the world which produced the innovations leading to industrial civilization were themselves cultural backwaters a fairly small number of generations earlier and their gene-pool is unlikely to have changed much.[33]

To sum up our argument, it does not follow from the fact that some ideas or technology originated in a particular society or culture that people belonging to different cultures must find it especially difficult to acquire or apply them. Indeed in certain circumstances, the contrary might be true. After all, even though techniques of settled agriculture, writing and urban living may have originated in Asia, there is little to suggest that a late start retarded European development. It is not at all obvious why any such special difficulty must exist for, say, Asian societies seeking to learn the techniques involved in modern economic growth. In justification of such a postulate, it could perhaps be plausibly argued that the experience of the recent past is binding but that of the more remote past is not, but such an argument would hardly be acceptable to historians, and even less so to archaeologists. There are, indeed, specific features of some existing societies which make economic development difficult to achieve, but that is a proposition of a quite different sort.

2.3 Does Economic Growth Lead to Cultural Decline?

I have been arguing against various types of cultural determinism. I want now to criticize a position of the opposite kind, one which implies that cultural factors, far from determining economic variables, are determined by them. On this view, cultures are not rigid, robust or overpowering, but on the contrary are apt to be buffeted about by winds of economic change. The problem then is not that cultural barriers constrain economic growth in less developed countries, it is rather that economic growth in such countries may have an adverse effect on their culture. 'Dependency theories' have often criticized the process of economic growth in developing countries on the ground that it makes them dependent on the West in respect both of technology and consumption patterns.[34] Such theories usually combine justified anger at neo-colonial exploitation with an almost mystical faith in the virtues of pre-industrial society and technology. A 'cultural' version was recently stated by a leading archaeologist. Modern economic growth, argues Clark,[35] is harmful to developing countries because it leads to a substitution of Western culture for their own. National performance, he observes, increasingly tends to be measured by the ' . . . extent to which the delights of the consumer society, identified with Western culture, are available to populations whose own indigenous cultures had until recently enriched the world' (p. 159). This, it is argued, leads in turn to a lowering in quality of the world's culture as a whole, to anonymity, homogenization and a loss of diversity.

The proposition that economic development leads to cultural decline can be differently interpreted depending on what, precisely, 'culture' is taken to mean. Development, by definition, implies change. Economic development, whether past or present, usually involves among other things the transformation of a predominantly agricultural society into a predominantly industrial one. Such a process must bring about changes in consumption patterns and life styles. What Clark describes as the 'homogenizing' effect of economic growth is, essentially, its tendency to iron out differences in life styles. Economic development in Third World countries, it is feared, will lead to people of these countries giving up their own food, dress, art, music, modes of behaviour and so on and adopting the predominant Western patterns instead, along with Western technology. Behaviour of this kind is certainly not unknown, especially among members of 'elite' groups in backward countries; but it is precisely under conditions of economic stagnation, especially when accompanied by colonial domination, that it has usually been found to occur. Nineteenth-century Bengal and twentieth-century French Africa provide well-known examples.

Independence and economic development have in fact brought about a reverse trend. People of developing countries have not only sought to preserve life styles characteristic of their culture, they have carried them abroad when emigrating. A typical resident of London, Paris or New York probably enjoys greater opportunities today for encountering or appreciating other cultures than ever before. The world-wide spread of the process of development has increased, not diminished, the variety of life styles. But quite apart from the facts of the matter, the *logic* of the argument is far from compelling, for if a change in cultural practices does occur, it need not necessarily portend a decline.

The process of industrialization may lead to the loosening of taboos, a relaxation of social pressures on individual conduct, and give a first taste of freedom to those at the bottom of the caste or ethnic ladder. As I have argued above, the resulting changes in modes of consumption or behaviour may be regarded as desirable for individuals, and hence for society.

Culture may also be interpreted in a different way, to denote certain aspects of feelings, beliefs, values, norms and outlook that are of a relatively stable or permanent nature. These are, presumably, what one refers to when describing the puritanical ethic as responsible for the rise of capitalism or trying to explain Japan's economic success by its culture or ethos. Whether economic growth in developing countries constitutes a threat to culture in this sense is another matter. Cultures are not really that fragile, especially those of countries where ancient civilizations once flourished and were succeeded by a long period of stagnation. Some basic elements of culture and ethics are probably stable over time horizons commonly envisaged in the analysis of economic change. Otherwise, they could not properly be invoked in explaining economic change at all. To the extent that they are stable, the assumption that economic factors do not significantly influence non-economic factors (discussed in chapter 1, section 1.4) continues to hold, and standard economic analysis applies. There are other factors in culture which are not quite so stable but which are capable of being successfully adapted to changing circumstances. They provide an area where individuals from developing countries can borrow from the West, improvising as they carry on; and this is what many of them have been doing. In technology as in culture, the ability to borrow is less a threat than an opportunity. It is the advantage of a late start.

I shall conclude this chapter with the following observation. Individual preference orderings do have a social dimension, and it is important for economists to recognize this. But this does not make the fulfilment of individual preferences less relevant as a yardstick of social wellbeing. I have argued above that in fact, the contrary is true. Nevertheless, individual preferences are not the *only* possible basis for measuring social wellbeing. Some others, which I believe are just as legitimate, will be examined in the next chapter.

3

The Justification of
Social Indicators

> Our basic needs are pretty straightforward – food, shelter, warmth,
> sex, prestige, in that order.
>
> P. D. James, *A Taste for Death*

3.1 Introduction

I argued in the previous chapters that the central concern of
economics has always been the satisfaction of human desires for
things rather than things themselves. For this reason, the
rationale of economic theory is naturally stated in 'subjective'
rather than 'objective' terms. When an economist is evaluating
states of affairs, one can confidently predict that he will at some
stage invoke the extent to which desires are fulfilled as his
'ultimate' or 'basic' criterion of evaluation. The use of GNP as a
measure of social welfare itself rests on this criterion. On the
other hand, critics of the economic approach, and the use of
GNP in particular, are a motley crowd. They have been trying to
express concerns of many different kinds. For some of them the
validity of individual preference as a basis, even as *the* basis, of
the evaluation of social states is not the point of attack at all; their
worry is rather that inidividual preferences may not be
adequately reflected in GNP. This could be because there are
certain items which cannot be captured by statistics at all,
because the 'connectedness' of preferences may fail to apply to
them, or because conventional national income data wrongly
excluded some relevant items, while including others that are
not, and so on. Others emphasize that judging the welfare of a
group involves inter-personal comparisons, which cannot be
properly carried out without going beyond individual preference
itself.[1]

Quite distinct from these is a view, criticized in chapter 2, that would reject the focus on *individual* preferences and instead regard society as an organic whole, whose welfare is to be interpreted accordingly. There are yet other approaches which seek to retain the emphasis on the primacy of the individual but regard the fulfilment of individuals' needs or the preservation of their rights, as more important than preference satisfaction.

Evaluations of social states resulting from the various positions described could be quite different. However, the issues involved in different approaches have not usually been distinguished from one another in a systematic way. Instead, people have often pointed out various limitations of GNP and gone on to suggest appropriate modifications to GNP itself or the use of other indices which would help overcome these limitations in some degree. A proliferation of indices with the generic title of Social Indicators has been the result. Some of these indicators have a long ancestry. For example, historians, in assessing how far the standard of living of a particular society or a section of it improved during a given time period, often rest their case on what changes occurred in such things as the per capita consumption of (inter alia) bread, meat, sugar, tea or soap, the prevalence of urban slums, the incidence of disease and so on, without being directly concerned at all with the question of to what extent, if any, the people involved desired such change.[2]

Other statistics covering a much wider area of activity are increasingly used in a routine and ad hoc way by social scientists, national governments and international agencies in order to compare levels of development, or levels of living, in different countries, to assess the changes in these levels for a given country over time, to monitor socio-economic performance and so on. Specific justification for indicators used in terms of either desire fulfilment or some other principle is seldom provided. Rather the things or conditions indicated are deemed to be important in themselves. The same is true of attempts by economists to measure the incidence of poverty and malnutrition in less developed countries, and it is also the distinguishing feature of what a philosopher has recently called the Objective List Theory of deciding on what makes someone's life go best.[3]

Objective conditions can be of different kinds, although this does not imply that all must be taken into account for a comparison to be valid. Their relevance can only be judged in a specific context and bearing in mind what questions one wishes to ask. Even so, in any given context, saying certain objective conditions are relevant or 'important in themselves' can only mean that their justification is obvious. What kind of justification could properly be offered for using objective conditions as a basis for comparing standards of living is therefore a matter of some importance, but it is hardly discussed in any depth in the literature on social indicators, which has been concerned more with such things as the degree of statistical correlation between different indices, the construction of composite indices and so on. To present arguments bearing on this matter in a systematic way, provides the motivation for the present chapter. I should like to distinguish between justifications based respectively on desires, basic needs, rights and excellence. Sometimes a given set of objective conditions could be justified by some or all of these, but the conditions to be used could also vary according to the kind of justification offered.

We shall discuss below the four principles of justification mentioned above and some possible relationships between them (for example, is one subsumed under another, does one exclude another and so on). Justification by desires (individual preferences) which lies at the heart of the economic approach, has already been discussed in the previous chapters. The present concentrates on the other possible kinds of justification, namely basic needs, rights and excellence, which are considered respectively in sections 3.2, 3.3 and 3.4, while section 3.5 deals briefly with a residual category. A comment on the interpretation of desire-based indicators will be made before we turn to these. It was argued in chapter 1 that GNP itself is best interpreted as a desire-based indicator of the level of living. Other social indicators which are also interpreted in this way (i.e. as desire based) are therefore closest in spirit to the GNP measure, even though, for a variety of reasons, the concerns that they express may fail to be captured by GNP: for example, because they have a non–market component (e.g. health, knowledge), because they are related to such non-economic variables as family life (e.g. leisure) and so on. Indicators of this kind could be useful supplements to GNP precisely for this reason. We must, however, avoid confusing desire-based indicators with desire indicators. On the former approach, although the things in question justify their claim to attention by being desired by individuals, once they have been accepted as social indicators, the focus remains on the things themselves rather than feelings about them, i.e. on 'bills of goods', not indifference curves. This has an important consequence. If the relevant objective conditions ('goods') remain the same but the person experiencing them has now a more (or less) favourable attitude towards them, we should not, on this view, wish to say that his condition has improved (or deteriorated). On the subjective approach, we should.

3.2 Basic Needs

What constitutes 'basic needs' will figure prominently in the discussion below. For convenience of exposition, I shall start by using a working definition of basic needs, that by Streeten: 'in terms of minimum specified quantities of such things as food, clothing, shelter, water and sanitation that are necessary to prevent ill health, undernourishment and the like'[4]. However, even in a 'shortlist' we would include primary education and health care. For most people, and especially for people who have grown up in a society shaped by mass poverty, using the fulfilment of basic needs as a yardstick for measuring social wellbeing makes a direct and powerful appeal to moral intuition, in the sense that trying to justify its use by appealing to some other and higher level principle is felt to be not only unnecessary, but even perhaps a little odd. Some people, it is true, do not share this intuition. An example is Nozick,[5] who attacks certain statements by Williams concerning the distribution of medical care on the ground that they rest ultimately on the claim that society should make provision for the important needs of all of its members. The point of Nozick's criticism is that this claim itself remains unproven. Of course the statement that society should try to provide for the important needs of its members, could itself be understood in different ways.

Our present discussion is concerned with questions relating to judgements as between different states of affairs rather than to actions by which particular states of affairs could be brought about. Applying the Nozick argument to this context, what requires to be proved is simply the claim that a society in which the important needs of all its members are satisfied should be regarded as ranking above one in which they are not. If someone does not see why it should, it is difficult to think what kind of proof would convince him. On the whole, though, such an intuition is now widespread, and it is this that lies behind the increasing concern of recent work in development economics with issues related to basic needs. In particular it is this that explains attempts to compare standards of living in terms of the extent to which basic needs are met. Yet a number of objections continue to be raised against this approach. In this section, I propose to deal with those that are most commonly found in the literature.

I shall begin by answering an objection to needs-based criteria of wellbeing made by some philosophers, namely that needs are merely an instrumental concept.[6] It is said that one cannot possibly assess the validity of the statement 'A needs X' unless one knows what A is supposed to need X for; even that such a statement is meaningless. Hence, it is argued, the sensible response to a statement of need is always to ask what the need is for. But specifying the end state by virtue of which a need arises does not justify the end state itself. 'One cannot decide whether A needs X unless one knows what he is alleged to need it for; but one does not have to pronounce on the merits of the latter.'[7] For this reason, statements of need are, it is said, distinguished by their non-normative character. But the concept of social indicators underlying the present study is essentially normative. How then, can needs provide a basis for social indicators? The following considerations, in my view, make this objection untenable.

While a purely instrumental concept of needs is indeed quite common, others may be no less legitimate. If a claim based on needs, as distinct say, from wants or desires is relevant at all, the desirability of the end state from which the need is derived is by definition a necessary part of the argument. That such a view of needs is certainly one of its meanings in the ordinary language is suggested by the definition of need in Webster's dictionary as 'an urgent requirement of something essential or desirable that is lacking'. This is also the sense of need in which Milton, pressing the claims of improved education in England ('. . . for the want whereof this nation perishes . . . '), wrote: 'I neither ought nor can in conscience defer beyond this time both of so much need at once and so much opportunity to try what God hath determined' and again a little later ' . . . for that, which I have to say, assuredly this nation hath extreme need should be done sooner than spoken'.[8] An objection on very similar lines against the concept of needs was recently raised by Culyer[9] in the context of health services. Standard definitions of needs, states Culyer, all refer to the need for a service or a range of services. But these are merely instrumental means for the achievement of an ultimate end. The choice among them, for example more or fewer hospital beds, particular surgical or medical interventions and so on, is, or should be, mainly a technical and economic matter, for they are needed only in so far as the end or outcome of the use is needed. According to Culyer, speaking of needs in this way, i.e. applying the language of needs to instruments, 'encourages a particular form of sloppy thinking, namely a denial of the substitutability of alternative means in attaining an end or, at least, a denial of the legitimacy of considering that the most effective means of meeting an ultimate need may be "too" costly and that possibly to adopt a less effective means or a less comprehensive means, or indeed no means at all might be the proper course' (p. 14). It is quite true that on the standard (i.e. consequentialist) concept of needs, it is only the end or outcome that matters for the purpose of evaluation.

In evaluating states of affairs according to a standard of needs, the use of indices of means or inputs can therefore only be justified in special circumstances, considered subsequently in this chapter. It may well be the case that in the health services such special circumstances do not prevail. But the argument as stated by Culyer can itself hardly be described as decisive, for it is not just 'means' that are substitutable for one another; different 'ends' could be substitutable as well. Because of the scarcity of resources, the achievement of high levels of health care for instance, may require lowering educational standards (unless, of course, it is attained at zero cost, in which case resources are not scarce). Indeed Culyer implies as much when, at the end of the sentence quoted, he suggests that adopting no means at all might be the proper course, for presumably in this case the 'outcome' would fail to be attained as well. The argument that the opportunity costs of different alternatives must be considered before a rational decision can be arrived at is entirely correct, but this is not the same as saying that ends and means are distinct.

Another criticism of basic needs as a principle for the evaluation of social states concerns its overlap with other principles. This view, while conceding the obvious merits of the basic need principle, would claim that those really of substance are already covered by such familiar categories as individual preferences, equality, redistribution with growth and the reduction of poverty. Hence, it is argued, the basic needs principle is unnecessary. Thus, it has been suggested that basic needs are not only related to, but should also be defined in terms of, individual preferences, namely as a particular set of desires. It is such an interpretation that underlies the concept of 'felt needs' (some comments on which are made later in the specific context of health care). As Streeten observes 'Basic needs may be interpreted subjectively as the satisfaction of consumer's wants as perceived by the consumers themselves . . . '.[10] This is perhaps too broad a description. More specifically, basic needs may be interpreted as simply another name for 'basic' desires, those coming at the top of a consumer's hierarchy of wants; food, clothing, shelter and so on. If we suppose a consumer starts from a position of zero resources, and subsequently acquires some, these are the desires he may be expected to try to satisfy first, before turning to others. Accordingly, basic needs would represent a bundle of goods and services for which low-income consumers would show very high income-elasticity of demand. Such an interpretation appears to underlie a widely used approach to the measurement of poverty, i.e. a state where basic needs fail to be met. On this approach, a poverty line is determined as the cost, at given prices, of acquiring a certain bundle of ('essential') goods and services. Those with an income below this level are said to be in poverty since they cannot afford to buy the bundle in question, while those with an income higher than this could buy it if they so desired.

The interpretation of basic needs in terms of desire is also not inconsistent with linguistic usage, which sometimes fails to distinguish between the need for an object and the desire for it. Words such as hunger and thirst generally refer *both* to a deficiency (lack of food or water) and the corresponding desire (to eat or drink).[11] (This is not true, however, of words such as malnutrition or vitamin deficiency: a person suffering from either may not necessarily desire that it should cease forthwith. He may even be unaware of his deficiency.)

While this interpretation has a certain plausibility, it is open to powerful objections. First, the priority of desires may not in practice match that emphasized by the 'basic needs' concept. To take an obvious instance, there are many individuals with meagre resources who proceed to spend a large part of any acquired income on alcoholic drinks; estimated income elasticities of demand for alcoholic beverages among low-income groups in some developing countries have been found to be extremely high. Yet one may not wish to define alcohol as a basic need for the individuals concerned (or their families). Conversely, there are certain goods and services (clean water, elementary education, primary health care) that are usually regarded as basic needs but which, even in the most 'laissez-faire' of societies, are seldom marketed. Expenditure patterns would give little information on individuals' desires, or needs, for such goods.

Secondly, even in cases where such discrepancies do not arise, the interpretation of basic needs as basic desires raises the following logical difficulty. Sorting out 'basic' desires from others is not something that can be done on the basis of the concept of preference alone, for the basicness of desires must rest on some notion of urgency, which is not itself a necessary part of the meaning of preference. In terms of economic analysis, a natural way of introducing 'urgency' into the picture would be via the consumer's willingness to pay, which also depends on his income. But in the case of goods or services included under the rubric of 'basic need', measuring urgency by willingness to pay could be inappropriate. A better alternative is to incorporate the notion of urgency into the concept of basic needs itself. Indeed it is the 'urgency', understood in an objective sense, of people meeting their basic needs that provides the concept of basic need with its essential moral core.

These considerations, in my judgement, justify regarding the 'basic need' principle as a principle in its own right, distinct from that of individual preferences. On the other hand, the two principles are complementary and, if carefully applied, may be expected to have a considerable overlap. In particular, from the consideration that needs are distinct from preferences, it does not follow that we are not entitled to take account of preferences in assessing or estimating needs. Suppose, for instance, that we are computing the cost of a diet ensuring an adequate nutritional level, as a step towards the construction of a poverty line. Suppose also that this is being done for a vegetarian community. It would be odd to argue that the preference for vegetarian food should *not* be taken note of, since this is a charactristic of wants rather than of needs (which relate to nutrition), while the claim that 'a vegetarian is in a sense always hungry'[12] can only be described as bizarre. More generally, while remaining within a needs approach, one could incorporate some aspects of preferences for particular items or kinds of goods fairly easily into the calculations without necessarily becoming trapped in methodological inconsistency. In the case of the 'optimum diet' problem, for instance, some constraints imposed by tastes could be added in quite a straightforward way to the constraints specifying that minimum nutritional requirements should be met, and the cost minimized subject to the constraints taken together. A number of such exercises have in fact been undertaken, which are useful in the sense that the basket of goods and services that is taken to represent basic needs is more acceptable to the individuals concerned and hence policies towards the satisfaction of needs based on them are likely to be more successful.[13] Some other instances of the fact that individual preferences and basic needs are complementary rather than mutually exclusive principles will emerge in the course of our subsequent discussion.

Let us now consider whether the fulfilment of basic needs could reasonably be subsumed under 'redistribution with growth'. It is clear at the outset that if this enterprise is to succeed, redistribution cannot be interpreted literally, for the satisfaction of certain basic needs creates non-redistributable assets; literacy is an obvious example. More promising is the argument that the case for basic needs is derived from that for equality. The minimalist character of basic needs for example could be explained by the argument that the most urgent needs of *all* should be ranked above less urgent wants of some. The idea of basic needs or 'human' needs is indeed ultimately linked to that of human equality in some sense, but the two are not identical. Mass illiteracy is, per se, not less egalitarian than mass literacy. Similarly, as between a society where everybody is starving and one where nobody is, the degree of equality is just the same.[14] If, nevertheless, one wishes to rank a society where everybody can read and write, above one where nobody can and a society where nobody starves above one where everybody does, this cannot be attributed to a preference for equality. Such a ranking is explicable only if the satisfaction of the basic need concerned is valued as such.

The conceptual links between the satisfaction of basic needs and the removal of poverty are stronger. Poverty itself is commonly measured as the proportion of the population whose level of consumption falls below a 'poverty line' given as the cost in constant prices of a basket of goods and services that would enable basic needs to be met. If this is the definition of poverty used and the basket included represents the needs one would wish to regard as basic, the satisfaction of basic needs must, by definition, occur at the point at which poverty disappears. But other definitions of poverty may also be no less relevant, and whichever definition of poverty one uses, one may still be justified in being concerned with particular basic needs regarded individually. Morally, the notion of satisfying basic needs may also be regarded as at least as compelling as that of removing poverty, for one thing, because whether basic needs are actually met is not necessarily a less important question than whether they are enabled to be met.

Finally, it could be argued that, regarded as a 'primitive' notion, the concept of basic needs is no less 'familiar' than that of equality and/or poverty and perhaps much more so than redistribution!

An objection against emphasizing needs rather than wants that has often been made by writers of a 'liberal' persuasion is that this would encourage attitudes of passivity at one end of the scale and 'dirigisme' at the other. Passivity, it is said, must always result when importance is given to what has been done for people, rather than what they have achieved by their own efforts. But such an objection could be made to any standard consequentialist evaluation which considers end states only to the exclusion of how an end state is reached. This cannot therefore be an issue between want-based and need-based approaches to the choice of social indicators. Its importance lies rather in reminding us that in comparing levels of social wellbeing, such matters as the extent of participation in decision making and the preservation of human dignity, which tend to get left out in consequentialist evaluation, could also be relevant. Such issues can perhaps be more conveniently discussed within a rights framework, which I shall deal with later.

The objection that an approach based on the concept of needs breeds dirigisme, i.e. it is inherently authoritarian, is related to the role of the State in knowing and fulfilling our needs. This is clearly stated by Little:[15]

Early on it seems to have been envisaged that basic needs could actually be defined in an appropriate and operational manner; and that governments should then set about, in some direct and dirigiste but essentially unspecified manner, ensuring that every family has so many calories, shelter of an approved standard, all children in primary school, and so on. The suspicion of excessive dirigisme and paternalism (implicit in the word 'needs') antagonized some liberals.

These two charges against the concept of needs, namely 'passivity' and 'dirigisme', appear to be linked, and both arise from a common underlying idea, namely that the satisfaction of wants or desires through the earning and spending of income represents the culmination of an *active* process (a process based essentially on the pursuit of self-interest) whereas the satisfaction of basic needs comes from people *passively* receiving benefits from the State. This idea, popular though it is, rests on a number of confusions. First, people who have made good in a market economy are not necessarily people of an up and doing or hyperactive kind. Let us consider a society where the allocation of resources is done as far as possible through the market mechanism, while the State confines its activities to the 'traditional' role of the maintenance of law and order and makes no conscious or deliberate effort to satisfy the basic needs of the people. Suppose also that there are a number of people in this society who have high levels of income and wealth and who are because of this in a position to satisfy their wants. The high level of satisfaction of their wants (and presumably of their needs as well) does not necessarily reflect an active disposition. Some of them could well be prudent, active, energetic people, who took their studies seriously from an early age, acquired useful skills, worked hard and well and saved regularly in working life. Others in their ranks might be people who simply had the luck to be born into a rich family and who have done nothing more active in their entire life than waiting patiently for the death of an aunt. The 'market' could reward them just as much! Unfortunately, given a particular population of the affluent, the economist has no means of telling how many of them belong to the one category and how many to the other. There are, however, some detailed empirical studies of the extent to which the actual inequality of wealth in a society can be ascribed to inheritance as opposed to one's own earnings, and these do show that inheritance has traditionally been the predominant factor. Even in a welfare state such as contemporary Britain, the contribution of inheritance to inequality continues to be a significant one.[16]

Given the right initial conditions, 'passivity' could be highly rewarding. Contrariwise, the extent to which basic needs are satisfied cannot be explained simply in terms of what the State did or did not do. Even at the stage of development of technology that the twentieth-century world has reached and however extensive the role of the State in economic activity, basic needs of the masses of the people in any society are not likely to be satisfied without long and strenuous efforts by them to influence the policies of the State in this direction. The process of satisfaction of basic needs is not like a gathering of manna by a thankful populace who live happily ever after. Looking back at the fairly recent past of countries that now rank as developed, the first steps taken by the State to satisfy some of the basic needs of the people appear often to have been inspired less by benevolence than by a fear of public disorder;[17] and the same is true of the developing countries today.

Criticisms against the basic-needs criterion of the kind voiced by Little, fail to distinguish clearly between two distinct groups of questions that are involved, namely those that arise in choosing between actions and those relevant to judging states of affairs. When one talks about a basic-needs strategy, it is the former that is being directly referred to, but our concern is with the latter. That the government of a country follows a basic-needs strategy does not necessarily imply that basic needs of the people are being met. Contrariwise, a government committed ostensibly to a quite different strategy, such as growth, may succeed in achieving both its primary objective and the satisfaction of basic needs of its people: the experience of Singapore provides a case in point.

Labels attached to policies may also be misleading, i.e. the kind of policy a government professes to follow may be quite different from what is actually followed. This may have some bearing on the validity of criticisms of 'basic needs' made from a liberal standpoint. As regards policies followed by governments of some less developed countires, 'dirigiste' may not perhaps be the *mot juste*: 'cruel', 'tyranical' or 'corrupt' could be more appropriate. It would be naive to suppose that the nature of these policies or of the governments pursuing them had much to do with a concrn for people's basic needs. The political imperatives were often quite different, the dominant 'basic need' being to ensure the survival of the regime. And far from antagonizing Western liberals, such policies frequently gained their approval, thus helping regimes of this kind to survive. To pursue issues of this kind further would however take us beyond the scope of this book. The relevant point is that arguments that would attribute guilt by association to the basic needs principle are quite unconvincing.

None of these objections to regarding the fulfilment of basic needs as a standard for the evaluation of social states appears to us to have much force. Some, as we have seen, are not really concerned with the evaluation of states of affairs at all. Others are simply mistaken. That much discussion of 'needs' has been careless and slipshod is true enough, but to conclude from this as Culyer does, that 'the word "need" ought to be banished from discussion of public policy' is hardly rational. If one is to shun all words that have been misused, one could not speak at all. I proceed to look briefly at some issues that arise in *determining* basic needs. The first such issue I shall discuss is, who is to determine one's needs. Since it is in the context of health-care needs that this matter has been most extensively discussed, I shall use that context to illustrate the argument.

The first question that arises is whether an individual is himself the appropriate person to decide his own needs. The notion that he is, is central to the argument of those writers who maintain the primacy of 'felt needs' and/or the validity of self-diagnosis.[18] Felt need can be regarded as simply another name for a want or desire, and in principle, we could attempt to evaluate a state of affairs in terms of the extent to which they are satisfied. However, instead of trying to approximate the degree of desire satisfaction using measures of real per capita consumption (the standard procedure favoured by economists), we could simply ask the population concerned through a well-designed sample survey. When assessing the need for a 'service', as Bradshaw[19] puts it, 'the population is asked whether they feel they need it'. The chief objection raised by critics of this approach is, as in the general case, that individuals may not always be in a position to assess their needs correctly and that even if they do, they may not be able to express their needs in an effective way. According to one of the most trenchant of such critics, Professor Titmuss, 'There are some needs which cannot be self-diagnosed; for medical care for instance, or mental health services or rehabilitation services. There are some needs which, though they are felt needs, are not expressed because of ignorance on the part of the individual that services exist and that anything can be done to mitigate or remove the need'.[20] Research shows, according to Titmuss, that unmet and unexpressed needs exist particularly among the poor, the badly educated, the old, those living alone and other handicapped groups. Yet these are often the people with the greatest needs. In other words, whether because of a failure on the part of people belonging to such groups in respect of the ability to feel their needs or the ability to express their felt needs, the needs concerned could not be known by decision makers and hence would not be met. The felt needs principle does not therefore carry us far enough.

The 'standard' view of the determination of needs in the literature of health economics has, on the other hand, always been that they are determined by the expert. This view rests on the belief that the individual himself cannot properly assess his needs, but an expert can. Indeed, it is the ability to do this, by virtue of training and experience, that makes someone an expert. Therefore, it is the expert's opinion which decides whether something counts as a need. Need is thus identified with 'normative' as opposed to 'felt' need and regarded as 'that which the expert or professional, administrator or social scientist defined as need in any given situation'.[21] A desirable or normative standard is derived on the basis of such a definition and the actual existing position compared with the norm. If for an individual or group the existing level of the attribute in question (whether this refers to the amount consumed of some good or service or a characteristic such as the nutrient level associated with it) falls short of the norm, the individual/group concerned is said to be in need and the degree of it measured by the extent of shortfall.

One could also take a view somewhere in between these two concepts of need, namely between one based on its expression by the individual concerned and the other defined in terms of an expert's judgement. One such position appears to be implied in the last two sentences in the passage from Titmuss quoted above. If, as Titmuss believes, it is ignorance on the part of the individual that stands in the way, it is surely plausible to suppose that even though an individual may not be able to determine his needs entirely on his own, given access to relevant information, time to reflect on his situation, opportunities for discussion with others, possibly counselling by an expert and so on, he may be able to do so at a reasonable level of competence. Conceptually, we then have a half-way house. Yet another kind of 'mixture' between the two concepts has been suggested by Cooper.[22] 'Needs are those demands, which in the opinion of the doctor require medical attention. That is they are an expert's view of our health state.' This, in effect, sets a twofold criterion. For an individual to be correctly described as being in (medical) need, he must actually demand some medical service, and his demand must also be 'certified' by a doctor. A number of studies suggest, however, that the demand recorded in this way may reflect the current supply of health care facilities rather than the extent of need.

Finally, it is possible that neither felt need nor expert opinion could suffice to determine a need. That an individual may not be able to diagnose his own needs does not necessarily mean that there must be someone else who can do this for him. Culyer states that from the passage from Titmuss quoted above, we may infer that 'since many of the most important needs are not expressed by those in need, they must be being expressed by someone else (in the limit, if only by Professor Titmuss)'. Such an inference appears unwarranted, for it may be the case that certain needs may not be capable of being determined (or 'expressed') by those in need nor, given the state-of-the-art, by an outside expert. But even in such a case, a statement asserting the existence of unsatisfied needs is not necessarily meaningless. The failure to diagnose does not suffice to make a patient healthy, though of course it does make it extremely difficult to understand how one could attempt to make him so!

This survey, brief as it is, of the state of the debate on the determination of needs is enough to bring out that the state is far from satisfactory. The reason for this is, I believe, that too much importance has been given to the question of who knows our needs. The discussion above suggests that it is not so much *who* knows our needs but rather *how* they are known that really matters. Moreover, the question is not, strictly speaking, so much a matter of knowledge as of judgement. In trying to explain the distinction between wants and needs, it was observed earlier that determining needs necessarily involves taking a great many circumstances into account and that this simply cannot be done by means of direct perception or intuition alone. This, it was argued, explains why an individual may not necessarily be the best person to decide what he needs. But the observation that determining needs is a complex affair does not cease to be true just because it is an outside expert rather than the individual himself, who is responsible for their determination. A doctor may perhaps in some instances decide what a patient's needs are just by looking at him, but frequently, this is not the case. In general, needs will require to be examined, assessed, judged.

Saying that something is a matter of judgement, rather than knowledge, is a step in the right direction, but it does not carry us far, for not all judgements are of equal merit: some are better than others, while some may not be any good at all. The question arises therefore, what makes a judgement generally acceptable. If the question is asked at this level of generality, useful answers are not, it is true, likely to be forthcoming, for judgements are of different kinds. Which arguments would be regarded as convincing or even as relevant depends to some extent on what kind of judgement we are considering. Legal, moral and aesthetic judgements tend to be supported by different sets of arguments, and when we are concerned with the assessment of needs in a practical context, elements of all three might be involved. Empirical judgements on matters of fact would be involved as well. Nevertheless, for any judgement, whatever the sort of judgement it is, to be acceptable, certain minimum requirements must always be satisfied. This is reflected in the common language. A judgement, irrespective of the specific issues that are being judged, which is found unacceptable is likely to be described as biased, arbitrary, whimsical, even quixotic, hasty, one-sided, narrow-minded, unfair and so on. Judgements regarded as good tend to be characterized as balanced, wise, expert, sound, far-sighted, comprehensive, according to the evidence, fair, equitable, humane and so on. We would deplore judgements that are clouded by passion or perverted by self-interest. If such are the judgements that tend to be made, we may even lament that judgement is fled to brutish beasts and men have lost their reason.[23]

I believe that linguistic usage has something important to teach us here; namely that characteristics of 'good' or 'acceptable' judgements relate predominantly to both how they are arrived at and to their consequences. Who sits in judgement can itself be regarded as a part of the process of how a judgement is said to be arrived at – in questions relating to procedural justice such an element is, indeed, often involved – but its significance is only derivative and hence secondary. This does not mean that getting the right sort of person to sit in judgement in any particular instance is a matter of little importance. Often it may be crucially important, for good judgements might fail to emerge otherwise. The two questions, *who* is to assess needs and *how* are they to be assessed, are thus not entirely unrelated. To take an obvious instance, if an interested party, i.e. someone who stands to gain or lose by the outcome is himself in charge of the business of assessment, a suspicion of bias in the concepts or procedures applied can easily arise. The judgement of an expert on the other hand is likely to be accepted *tout simple* as an expert judgement.

An expert's judgement is not, of course, immune to the possibility of bias arising from self-interest. Doctors, in particular, especially in a regime of private medicine, have often been accused of choosing a particular treatment (such as surgery) not on grounds of the patient's need but because it is more profitable to the doctor; but in all societies the individual is given some protection against such practices by accepted codes of professional ethics. A generalized suspicion of the expert of a less specific kind, is also often associated with commitment to a democratic culture. A recent instance of it occurs in the study of poverty in contemporary Britain by Mack and Lansley,[24] who suggest that the assessment of minimum needs, which has historically been made by experts, tends to suffer from a conservative bias because they have much to lose from a redistribution of resources in society, and even that 'the judgments being made by the professionals reflect their own interests rather than those of society generally' (p. 64). Accordingly, they are in favour of an approach which removes the concept of minimum needs and hence that of poverty 'from the arbitrary exercise of judgement by "experts", politicians and governments where up to now it has remained firmly entrenched and opens it up to a more democratic representation of interests' (p. 47). But this could well lead to an increase in, rather than a correction of, the 'conservative bias' in assessment of minimum needs.

A more important source of mis-specification of needs by an expert could be that even if he has no special interest in the outcome, he could well have an interest in the methodology to be used for arriving at an outcome. He may for instance have made his academic reputation by developing a particular method and may now be committed to it, regardless of whether it is relevant to prevailing circumstances, whether it has been made obsolete by new knowledge and so on. The point really is that in the context of assessing needs, the *how* question and the *who* question are different, and the value of the latter is essentially of an *instrumental* kind. A little cloak of authority cannot in itself ensure the acceptability of judgements.

The assessment of needs, that of basic needs in particular, involves ascertainment of facts (e.g. how many calories does a man require?) as well as rational argument (e.g. in determining which facts are relevant for deciding on a particular outcome). For both of these, the opinions of specialists are indispensable but such opinions nevertheless are subject to analysis, argument and debate. These may, in turn, have a feedback effect on the views of the specialists themselves, for in the course of defending their opinions against those of other experts, whether from their own or from other fields, or even against criticism by members of society at large, they may come to have a deeper understanding of the reasons for disagreement: whether these arise from differences concerning matters of fact, the underlying assumptions of their 'model', the basic value judgements and so on. In some cases, such debate could even act as a spur to experts to find out more about the issues at stake, and as a result, our knowledge about them may improve and at least *some* differences of opinion may come to be resolved. This account of the matter may appear idealized, over optimistic or even naive to those who doubt if 'real' progress, whether material or intellectual, ever occurs, but the recent debate on protein–calorie deficiency is a good practical instance. Because of recognition by experts of the fact that at low levels of calorie intake, protein itself tends to be 'burnt up', i.e. used in effect as calories, calorie requirements rather than those of protein have now come to be accepted as the crucial element of basic needs as far as nutrition is concerned.[25]

Another important question is whether needs are properly interpreted in absolute or in relative terms. In the presentation so far, the criterion of needs has been sought to be justified by the absolute necessity for certain (basic) needs being fulfilled in order that an individual may survive at all or that he may function effectively and with dignity as a human being. An 'absolute' notion of needs underlies this approach. Some have always argued, on the contrary, that needs are essentially relative, though they do not always hold the same view on what needs are relative to. The distinction itself is not a clear-cut one.

The specification of nutritional needs in terms of amounts of calories and other nutrients required per day would probably be regarded as the typical instance of the 'absolute' aproach to needs; yet, these amounts are 'relative' to age, sex, body weight, the nature of work activity and so on. Also, between two healthy and active men with the same age, body weight and work activity the need for calories can vary because of metabolic differences between them; if the first individual is biologically more efficient, his need would be less. Even for the same individual the calorie intake required varies from one day to another.[26]

Basic needs of individuals for clothing and shelter are related to the climate in which they live, while health-care needs vary considerably with age, a point of much practical importance in societies with rising life expectancy. This is not, however, the kind of variation one usually has in mind when describing needs as being 'relative'. Further, regarding basic needs as 'absolute' does not imply regarding them as fixed in the sense of being invariant over time. Most people would agree that basic needs usually include both a permanent biological component and a historically and socially determined component changing over time, though they may disagree on just how important this latter component is as compared to other components, the extent and determininants of such change, how long it takes for a change to become effective and so on.[27]

The distinctive feature of the 'relative' as opposed to an 'absolute' concept of basic needs is rather that on the former view, in a given society at a given time, what an individual needs is thought to be determined by what others actually have. Hence, on this view, the extent of poverty, i.e. the extent to which basic needs fail to be met, is naturally expressed in terms of relative deprivation. An early expression of this view was by Crossland, who argued that only a relative view of poverty was tenable ' . . . since the unhappiness and injustice it created, even when ill-health and malnutrition are avoided, lies in the enforced deprivation not of luxuries, but of small comforts which others have and are seen to have . . . '.[28] More recently, Townsend has argued that 'poverty can be defined objectively and applied consistently *only* [italic added] in terms of relative deprivation'.[29] On his definition, people (individuals, families or groups) are said to be in poverty if 'they lack the resources to obtain the types of diet, participate in the activities and have the living conditions and amenities which are customary, or are at least widely encouraged or approved in the societies to which they belong' (p. 31). In effect, someone is said to be poor if his income and assets are so much below the average as to exclude him from ordinary living patterns, customs and activities enjoyed by others. The 'others', relative to whose standards one's needs are thus to be judged, are defined as those sharing the same culture (hence Crossland's reference to 'prevailing cultural standards', p. 89), belonging to the same society (as in Townsend's definition cited above) or residing in the same State (e.g. the Council of Europe's definition of the poor 'as those whose resources are so small as to exclude them from the minimum acceptable way of life of the Member State in which they live', EEC, 1981, quoted in Mack and Lansley, p. 41). That needs based on culture, on society and on State could be different has not been sufficiently recognized in the literature, and other ways of delimiting boundaries could also be thought of.

In the relativist accounts of basic need just described, no reference is made to the feelings of the needy; it is activities, customs, ways of living with which they are essentially concerned. There are some other versions of relativism which rely fairly heavily on the feelings associated with deprivation, shame being he feeling most commonly invoked in this context. Such interpretations start from the observation that a certain level of assets and consumption is commonly regarded as 'decent', i.e. as setting a minimum acceptable social norm. Those unable to meet the standards set suffer feelings of shame or inadequacy. The basket of goods and services included in the 'norm' is accordingly defined as basic needs.

The 'relativist' approach to basic needs involves some difficulties that have not been sufficiently recognized. This applies especially to its 'subjective' version. To recognize certain standards of consumption as socially approved by no means entails that one must suffer feelings of shame if one fails to attain them. Many other kinds of 'affect' are equally plausible. Suppose, for instance, that one lacks the means to obtain even such things as a bowl of rice for one's family, or medical attention for a child lying seriously ill or any shelter, so that one is forced to sleep on the street. Such a situation may well produce in those experiencing it, or even in a spectator, feelings of despair, sadness, disgust, anger, even a determination to bring about a society in which such things shall not be. With repetition, feelings may even be numbered altogether. In any event, shame is hardly the sentiment that springs to mind in such a context. The point is that in such instances it is hardly likely that there should be any difference of opinion on their labelling as needs. Whether one takes a relativist or an absolutist approach to needs makes little difference, for all would agree that in the instances cited, severe deprivation has occurred and the most fundamental basic needs have not been met. This is precisely the reason that writers who would define needs in terms of a feeling of shame do not usually refer to such 'extreme' or 'urgent' needs at all. They have been concerned with the problems of measuring the extent of poverty in societies where, as a result of economic development, extreme deprivation of this kind is now rare or non-existent. But even in such cases, an analysis of need in terms of customary or conventional standards of what it is one feels shame to be without, is by no means satisfactory.

Such a reading makes it difficult to distinguish in principle between the concept of need and that of socially determined individual preferences, discussed in chapter 1. Moreover, as pointed out there, an individual in a modern economically advanced society invariably belongs to a multiplicity of groups, with *different* customary or conventional standards of consumption behaviour; hence the practical usefulness of this approach for determining needs is also limited.

Finally, the observation that an account of need based on feelings of shame tends to be unduly restrictive continues to apply. Someone may, for example, be perfectly aware that his or her own levels of consumption or wealth are lower than what socially approved standards would require, but, at the same time, believe that these standards themselves are based on wrong values (because for example, they place too much emphasis on material comfort) or even that letting one's own needs or goals be dictated by custom, convention or social approval would be a denial of one's autonomy and erosive of one's self-respect. In the circumstances described, such a person, far from being ashamed that his levels of 'comfort' fall short of what society regards as proper, might feel amused, angered, saddened or embarrassed by his society's worship of false gods, relieved that he is no longer in the rat race or even proud and joyful at being different. Which particular feeling predominates would vary with the person and the society concerned. A subjective–relativistic account of needs based on notions of 'decency' and 'shame' rests however on far too simplistic a view of the nature of social existence in the modern world.[30]

The objective version of the relativist thesis looks more promising. Certain difficulties arise, though, in regard to the appropriate level of aggregation at which a conventional standard is to be defined. Supposing that basic needs are indeed determined by what others have, one can ask *which* others? The relevant groups could be much smaller than state, society or culture, and at a given time a wide variety of conventional standards is likely to exist. Typically, in a hierarchical society the higher up one is in the hierarchy, the greater one's needs would be deemed to be. 'Poverty' for each group could be computed accordingly. But many of us might regard such a concept of need as lacking a moral basis. In a world with so much economic inequality between nations, defining needs purely on a national basis appears to me to involve a similar difficulty. For practical purposes, given that nation–states are here to stay, using national boundaries for economic indices is not only useful, it is indispensable. Answers to questions of policy concerning income redistribution or poverty removal in advanced countries are, also, to a great extent independent of whatever levels of poverty in developing countries may happen to be. These are not, however, the questions that concern us here. What is at stake is whether at the level of the *conceptualizing* of basic needs, it can ever be right in principle to regard the state of extreme deprivation in which large segments of humankind still live as entirely irrelevant, for this is what the 'relative' view of poverty really implies. I believe that to do so is to negate the concept of a common humanity on which, I argued earlier, the justification of an evaluation of states of affairs by the fulfilment of basic needs ultimately rests.

To conclude, relativistic notions of poverty had a certain plausibility in status-bound feudal-type societies with a stagnant economy. In some such societies they have enjoyed not only social but even legal sanctions. In some medieval Italian cities, for instance, a man whose status obliged him to keep servants was defined legally to be poor if, because of straitened circumstances he had to reduce the size of his retinue.[31] In today's world, whether in developing or developed societies, such notions appear much less plausible. The concerns which they seek to express are more appropriately dealt with by the concepts of absolute deprivation on the one hand and relative inequality on the other. Distinguishing between the two is more conducive to clear thinking than using a 'relative' definition of poverty according to which there may well be greater poverty in Britain than in Bangladesh and more poverty in Britain in the 1980s than in the 1880s, while a concept of need that makes the individual subject to 'the tyranny of the prevailing opinion and feeling'[32] must be deemed to be seriously deficient from the moral point of view.

3.3 Rights

The level of wellbeing of a society could also be judged in terms of rights rather than wants or needs. Economists, it is true, have not been as a rule greatly concerned with rights as a component of the standard of living. It is differences in social welfare, arising from how far individuals' desires are fulfilled, that have traditionally claimed their attention, and the discussion in chapter 1 suggests that they have also been pre-occupied with the question of basic needs to a far greater extent than has usually been supposed. Rights on the other hand have been emphasized mostly by those writing on law, ethics and political science. Yet, in recent writings on welfare economics, the connection between rights and welfare has been regarded as of crucial importance, and the proposition that 'rights serve as criteria by which to judge social, economic and political arrangements'[33] would probably command much greater assent from economists now than would once have been the case. But there is yet no such agreement as to which particular rights could most appropriately serve as such criteria, even on what precisely a 'right' means. I shall start by considering some possible meanings.

There are a great many different concepts of what a right is. Indeed, much of the literature on rights consists of vehement attacks by philosophers and political theorists on concepts of rights held or implied by other philosophers and political theorists. Such an approach does not seem to be particularly useful, for there is no reason to believe that one all-purpose definition of rights must be *the* definition, all others being irrelevant, trivial or plain nonsensical. Different concepts of rights could be appropriate or useful in discussing different kinds of questions. The questions that concern us here are those that are relevant to the evaluation of states of affairs, 'social states' in particular.

Let us consider briefly a few of the concepts of rights that have been proposed in the literature which could be relevant in this context. There are, first, a group of definitions of rights, which, despite some differences among themselves, agree in their emphasis on the primacy of rights over other claims. Rights, as it were, are trumps. Let us take a few examples. Buchanan[34] would understand by a right, 'a moral entitlement which ought to be established by the coercive power of the state if necessary'. According to Fried,[35] rights are 'categorical moral entities such that the violation of a right is always wrong'. Dworkin[36] suggests that welfare should be maximized subject to certain rights, which belong inalienably to individuals. Nozick,[37] who provides the most systematic recent exposition of this point of view, regards rights as moral *constraints* on actions: 'Rights do not determine a social ordering but set the constraints within which a social choice is to be made, by excluding certain alternatives, by fixing others, and so on.' Nozick's description of rights here is perhaps too broad for it would apply as well to taboos, ordinary social conventions and so on, in that rights are not only moral constraints, they are also moral constraints which must on no account be violated. 'Individuals have rights and there are things no person or group may do to them (without violating their rights)' (p. IX). On the other hand, on this view rights do not count as part of the goal or end state to be achieved but only as constraints on them. As Nozick puts it 'The side constraint view forbids you to violate these moral constraints in the pursuit of your goals, whereas the view whose objective is to minimize the violation of these rights allows you to violate the rights (the constraints) in order to lessen their total violation in that society' (p. 29). In other words, each constraint, regarded separately, is binding. A constraint must not be violated even if doing so could lead to better consequences, and this holds even if the minimization of violations of constraints is itself reckoned as part of the consequences in question. Trade-offs between one right and another or between rights and other things are not permissible.

There is considerable overlap between some of these defini- tions. In particular, in *all* these versions, saying that A has a right to X is much more than saying X is good for A, or A ought to have X or a society that is capable of providing X to A, but does not do so, gets a 'negative score' for this reason when we are comparatively evaluating different societies, and so on. Buchanan's definition of rights appears to be somewhat different, for on the face of it he seems to be emphasizing the *legal* aspect of moral rights. But this would be a superficial view. The logic of his definition points in the same direction as Nozick's or Fried's; it is by virtue of being an absolute and categorical moral claim that something can be a right. This comes out more clearly if we look at Buchanan's own exposition of the nature of a right to a 'decent minimum'. 'The claim to a decent minimum', he states, 'is much stronger than the claim that everyone *ought* to have access to such a minimum or that, if they did, it would be a good thing or that any society which is capable, without great sacrifice, of providing a decent minimum but fails to do so is deeply morally defective. None of the latter assertions implies the existence of a right' (p. 57). The something 'extra' that a right must have is essentially that it must have an over-riding character; it must supersede other claims, such as those based on maximizing social welfare.

In referring to the 'coercive powers of the state, if necessary' Buchanan (and some others) is *not* as has sometimes been thought, proposing a new and additional criterion for rights to exist. He is simply stating in a rather dramatic way the absolute importance he attaches to rights being observed. Presumably in arriving at a judgement on whether or not coercive powers of the State *were* necessary for a right to be implemented, one would have to consider whether in the absence of such power, the right in question was likely to fail to be established; on the other hand, the availability of legal sanctions by the State does not necessarily guarantee that a right will be observed. One has only to think of the right to freedom of speech guaranteed by the constitution of the Soviet Union, or to equality before the law implicit in the American Declaration of Independence[38] to realize how wildly over-optimistic such a supposition would be. One could of course say of such cases that coercive powers are not being applied with enough vigour, the political will to implement the rights concerned is lacking and so on, but this does not give us any information about the validity of the rights themselves; furthermore, for the coercive powers in question to have independent cognitive status, they must be capable of being observed independently of whether or not the objective (implementation of rights) is attained.

Given that rights are to be regarded as over-riding other claims, there is still a distinction between those who regard rights as *constraints* and those who see them as part of the social ordering itself. As regards the former approach, Nozick, as we have seen, thinks of rights as setting the constraints within which a social choice is to be made. However, this is not so helpful when our immediate concern is with evaluating states of affairs rather than determining choices. A standard application of the theory of constrained optimization in economic analysis is consumer's choice with a budget constraint. If the quantities chosen at the given prices cost more than his budget, they would be rejected forthwith as infeasible: a solution must, at least, be feasible. By analogy, if a particular state of affairs is characterized by a violation of a right, i.e. to use Nozick's phrase it does not exclude an alternative which *must* be excluded, this state of affairs must also be 'rejected'. This could mean either that one refused to evaluate the state of affairs in question (which does not carry us far!) or that one regards it as wrong (whatever other characteristics it may have) and hence as inferior to any other state of affairs under consideration in which such violation does *not* occur. On this interpretation as well, the task of evaluation can make only very limited progress!

On the other version, of which the views of Fried and Buchanan cited above are typical, though rights are still given an over-riding character, they need not necessarily be seen as *constraints* on action. If this version is interpreted narrowly as characterizing the range of morally permissible actions (the violation of a right being by definition impermissible), it reduces to the constraint-based version already considered. Interpreted more loosely, it could be applied directly to evaluate states of affairs without necessarily giving rise to the conceptual difficulties encountered in that case. It has indeed been used in this way by some writers to provide a clear-cut answer to the question raised at the beginning of this section, namely *which* rights can approximately serve as criteria for evaluating states of affairs, and standards of living in particular. Their answer is that only negative rights qualify. Positive or welfare rights to a decent minimum, cannot, it is argued, properly be called rights at all because, unlike negative rights, they impose resource costs and these may be so high that, given the limited resources of the society concerned, such rights may not be implementable. The demands of practicability rule out positive rights. The argument is stated by Fried[39] as follows:

It is ligically possible to respect any number of negative rights without necessarily landing in an impossible and contradictory situation. . . . Positive rights, by contrast, cannot as a logical matter be treated as categorical entities because of the scarcity limitation. It is not just that it may be too costly to provide a subsistence diet to the whole Indian subcontinent in time of famine – it may be simply impossible. But it is this impossibility which cannot arise in the case of negative rights.

I shall make two comments on this statement. First, Fried's

example is not well-chosen, for it assumes that famines are simply due to a shortage of food. Recent work on famines has firmly established that this need not necessarily be the case. Famines often occur without any sharp decline in aggregate food production, which could even be *higher* than in a normal year.[40] Even if food production has declined, availability need not, because of the possibilities of trade and storage. And even in cases where food availability had declined, ensuring a minimum subsistence diet for everyone need not be physically impossible. The deprivation that occurs during a famine is often due not so much to a shortage in total food supply as such, as to a lack of entitlements on the part of certain groups of society to access to food; for example, lack of transport, inadequate assets, a drastic fall in the relative price of labour as compared to food and so on. Hence, for Fried's argument to hold, it must be the case that such vulnerable groups cannot possibly be provided with any such scheme of entitlements that would ensure their 'positive' right to a minimum diet in a famine year. There is little reason to believe in any such impossibility theorem. The experience of India, a major component of the Indian subcontinent to which Fried refers, is surely of much relevance here. It is a matter of record that no major crisis has been caused there by famines since the mid-1960s, and the evidence strongly suggests that this was achieved not so much by an increase in per capita food production (which does not in fact show any striking increase) nor by a levelling up of society at large, but largely by operating buffer stocks of food grains, resulting in more effective entitlement to food for the urban poor. That the decision makers concerned came to believe in the possibility of ensuring a minimum subsistence diet even if crops failed, itself played an important part in this achievement, limited as it is.

A more important point is that *all* rights, 'negative' or 'positive', involve resource costs. On any non-trivial definition the fulfilment of negative rights cannot be achieved by a society without resources being used for this purpose. Take such a simple negative right as to be able to go about one's business without being harassed or attacked on account, say, of the colour of one's skin, one's sex, caste or tribal origin and so on. The lower the extent to which this human right is violated in practice, the better off on this score a society would be deemed to be. But to achieve a reduction is not simply a matter of taking up a certain moral stance or of legislative enactment, but also of resource allocation. Given that resources are limited, more of one right could be achieved at the cost of achieving less of another. Hence in principle the concept of a Pareto frontier is just as applicable to rights as to individual preferences. This suggests a different approach to rights, to which we now turn.

So far, the discussion of rights has been solely in terms of definitions according to which the distinctive feature of rights is that the claims they represent necessarily over-ride all other claims. However, despite frequent assertions to the contrary in recent literature, this is *not* the only relevant concept of rights. There is an older school of thought in which rights and other outcomes have been regarded as valued goals. On this view, the question of trade-offs between rights and other goals, far from being logically excluded from consideration by the very definition of rights, is thought to be vitally important, for it is on the magnitude of such trade-offs that the relative evaluation of different social states will, in practice, depend. In essence this represents a consequentialist as distinct from a purely deontological view. The classic modern exposition of this view is Berlin's.[41]

For historical reasons, the concept of rights has been closely linked to that of individual freedom and those who would seek to judge social wellbeing inter alia by the extent to which rights are fulfilled, have naturally concentrated on the right to freedom in its traditional 'negative' sense of non-interference by others. One is normally said to be free, observes Berlin, to the degree to which no one interferes with one's activity. If one is prevented by other persons from doing what one wants, one is to that degree unfree and if the area within which one can do what one wants is contracted by other people beyond a certain minimum, one can justly be described as being coerced. However, in order that something may properly be described as coercion, it must be a constraint imposed by others. Coercion must not be used as a term which covers *every* form of inability. If someone is unable to jump more than 10 feet in the air or cannot read because of blindness or cannot understand the darker pages of Hegel, it would be eccentric, says Berlin, to describe his condition by saying that he is to that degree being coerced or enslaved. In the sense of freedom that Berlin regards as the relevant one, one lacks it if one is prevented from attaining one's goal by other human beings, not merely if one is unable to attain one's goal. While in his discussion of freedom, Berlin almost always uses the terms *political* freedom or *political* liberty, these words are also used without this qualification to convey the same general meaning. Freedom of speech and association, freedom from being assaulted, freedom from arbitrary arrest and so on are particularly important instances of freedom in this general and negative sense.

In principle one should be able to construct social indicators to represent the level of fulfilment of such freedoms and hence to compare societies accordingly. Practical problems could arise, e.g. definitions of such terms as free speech or arbitrary arrest are not obvious; in regimes which habitually violate such freedoms, collecting statistics about the extent of their violation could be quite hazardous and so on, but no new principle would seem to be involved. What requires examination is whether there are also *other* 'freedoms'. This requires us to examine the validity of claims for the satisfaction of basic needs, such as a minimum level of nutrition, shelter or health care, to be regarded as 'economic' or positive freedom, distinct from, but no less important than, freedom understood in its usual political or 'negative' sense.

Berlin's account of the matter is based on a twofold argument. First, incapacity to attain one's goal (e.g. to have one's basic needs satisfied) cannot in itself be equated with a lack of freedom; freedom is lacking only to the extent that one is prevented from attaining one's goals by other human beings, their institutions and devices. Hence, poverty can properly be described as a lack of freedom only by those who believe it to be a result of an unjust or unfair social arrangement, rather than being brought about either by some lack of mental or physical capacity of the poor themselves, such as blindness to revert to Berlin's own example, or by agencies other than human beings, as retribution for one's 'Karma' in a previous incarnation for example. Since this is indeed commonly believed by those who take up the cause of economic freedom (and it is difficult to see how they could plead that cause *without* believing this), it seems to follow that on this view of the society concerned, positive and negative freedom *are* conceptually similar. That Berlin nevertheless prefers that they should be distinguished, is due simply to the fact that in such a case the lack of ('economic') freedom is the result of a lack of 'justice' or 'fairness' in the social order; hence, it makes for greater clarity to point to the injustice or unfairness directly rather than use lack of freedom as a catch-all term.

The second and more important point is that individual freedom (i.e. freedom from interference) is not the only worthy human goal. There are also other goals with intrinsic moral value such as happiness, security, justice or equality. These need not always co-exist with freedom and if a conflict does arise, freedom is not necessarily the prior claim. To offer political rights or safeguards against intervention by the State to men who are half-naked, illiterate, underfed and diseased is, according to Berlin, to mock their condition; they need medical help or education before they can make good use of an increase in their freedom. And achieving this, i.e. satisfying basic needs of the people, may itself in certain historical circumstances, necessitate a sacrifice of 'freedom'. However, to recognize the possibility of a trade-off is quite different from saying that in such a case, although liberal individual freedom may go by the board, some other kind of freedom, 'social' or 'economic', would be increased thereby. Such a statement makes little difference to the substantive argument, about what states of affairs are to be regarded as desirable, but it greatly increases the chances of confusion.

Everything, Berlin reminds us, is what it is:

Liberty is liberty, not equality or fairness or justice or human happiness or a quiet conscience . . . . If the liberty of myself or my class or nation depends on the misery of a vast number of other human beings, the system which promotes this is unjust and immoral. But if I curtail or lose my freedom, in order to lessen the sum of such inequality, and do not thereby materially increase the individual liberty of others, an absolute loss of liberty occurs. (page 10)

This is so, even though it may be compensated by a gain in justice, happiness and so on. Clearly this is a consequentialist view in which both rights (to liberty) and other outcomes (in particular, basic need satisfaction) count as goals to be valued, and the possibility of a trade-off between them cannot be rejected a priori.

While Berlin's essay is remarkable, among other things, for its lucid analysis of the content of what is generally described as negative rights, it does not actually invoke the terminology of rights at all. For a broader understanding of the issues involved, it is helpful to have the logic of the argument developed, within an explicitly formulated rights framework. This has recently been done by Sen[42] in terms of what he calls a 'goal-right' system, i.e. a moral system in which the realization of certain rights is specifically included among the goals incorporated in the evaluation of states of affairs. From the point of view of our concerns in this chapter, two specific features of the goal-rights system are particularly important. For a system to qualify as a goal-rights system, it is *not* required that all goals are rights, only that some rights are goals. 'The crucial issue', as Sen puts it (p. 15) 'is the inclusion of fulfilment and non-fulfilment of rights, rather than the exclusion of non-right considerations in the evaluation of states of affairs.' Secondly, rights are not necessarily regarded as absolute, over-riding *other* claims. On the contrary, a goal-rights system admits the possibility of trade-offs between rights included as goals (i.e. as relevant in evaluating states of affairs) and other (rights or non-rights) goals.

The difference between a consequentialist and a deontological understanding of rights is about the substantive content of one's moral judgements. There are *many* things to which, as a rule, we ascribe moral value (as the passage quoted earlier from Berlin emphasized). In what order of moral importance we should arrange them, or whether there can be any such a priori order at all, are themselves questions concerning our moral judgements. To say that 'negative' rights to personal freedom are not just moral entities but *categorical* moral entities, while 'positive' rights to certain minimum or basic needs are not, is itself to take a certain moral position. It is equivalent to asserting a kind of lexicographic moral ordering over states of affairs. A state in which the negative right in question is honoured in the sense that there is no infringement of personal freedom beyond a certain stipulated or necessary minimum, is then always judged to be superior to a state in which such infringement occurs, irrespective of all other considerations, for example even if the former state of affairs is also characterized by the prevalence of mass starvation while in the latter, material basic needs are satisfied. This is indeed a position which some 'liberals' appear to profess, but it is an extreme stance to adopt.

The goal-rights view is not only more balanced and flexible, it is also much better adapted to the specific enterprise of evaluating levels of social wellbeing. Whether or not it is logically possible to regard negative rights as categorical is not, in any case, decisive, for one is not morally bound to do so, even if it is. Contrariwise, even if one believes that positive rights cannot logically be regarded as categorical, one may still be justified in giving them a great deal of importance in assessing states of affairs.

To sum up, I would favour a moderate/middle-of-the-way, rather than an extreme/fundamentalist, concept of rights as appropriate for the purpose of evaluating states of affairs. Both positive and negative rights could be relevant in this context. However, in view of the difficulties with 'rights' catalogued above, one may well ask if a rights-based approach to evaluation has much to offer, after all. In other words, does it make a difference to the actual business of evaluating different social states whether or not rights are explicitly introduced into the analysis? There are at least two important ways in which it *could* make a difference. First, even though I differ from those rights theorists who in every possible circumstance would give absolute priority to the 'negative' right of political liberty above all other considerations, I believe 'negative' human rights to be extremely important. In many less developed countries, with whose levels of living we are primarily concerned in this book, serious violations of the rights of individuals have become all too common. This is especially true of the human rights of women. As well, individuals belonging to particular political, religious, caste, tribal, linguistic or ethnic groups have been and are discriminated against, persecuted, sometimes massacred in large numbers without even a semblance of protection by the State. While journalists, political commentators and civil rights groups have often drawn the world's attention to such events, they hardly ever get even a passing mention in the literature of development economics. Yet they are surely of great importance if we are serious in wishing to derive a realistic assessment of social wellbeing or levels of living. In the context of evaluating social states taking rights seriously provides us with a means of giving such considerations their due.

Secondly, in choosing social indicators of wellbeing, taking rights into account could make an important difference by giving respectability to input-based indicators. If we are concerned solely with the fulfilment of desire or of basic needs, only *results* count. Hence, measures of output provide the appropriate indicators. Using input-based measures, for example primary enrolment ratio as an indicator of the level of primary education achieved, or the number of hospital beds or doctors per head as an indicator of health, then requires special justification. Consider some of the arguments that have been used for this purpose. The one most widely used is that the outputs concerned cannot be easily measured, hence we may use inputs as proxies. This implies outputs *can* be ('easily') measured in terms of inputs, and is thus contradictory. Alternatively, the argument could mean that outputs cannot be easily measured *except* by using inputs as a proxy. In this case, we cannot possibly judge that such use will lead to valid indicators of results achieved. The argument must, therefore, be rejected.

A more credible argument for justifying the use of input-based indicators within a desire fulfilment (or basic needs) framework is that inputs are roughly proportional to outputs. This could be true, for example, if returns to scale are constant and there are no serious differences in the efficiency of resourse use between the situations being compared. Neither condition appears to hold in the production of 'inputs' in fields such as health and education. Whether we are using input- or output-based social indicators (or for that matter, GNP), an average over a group of persons cannot do the job of the distribution itself. This difficulty may be especially acute for input measures such as per capita availability of hospital beds because these may be concentrated in urban areas so that an increase in the figure for the region as a whole may not actually mean that the rural people are better served, and similarly, if investment is made increasingly in village-level primary health-care services rather than, as before, in hospitals, the number of hospital beds per capita may fall, even though rural people actually have access to improved health care (which appears to have happened since the 1960s in Indian Punjab).[43] It is less likely to be a problem for such output-based social indicators as per capita calorie consumption, literacy or life expectancy at birth, where the effect of 'better' levels enjoyed by a privileged group in pushing up the overall average cannot be quite so pronounced.

Clearly, from either a desire or a basic needs point of view, the use of input-based measures can only rarely be justified. If, however, our concern is primarily with rights, the emphasis which such measures place on the provision of opportunities rather than the actual level of use which people make of them is entirely as it should be. On a rights-based morality, the use which people make of the opportunities open to them are essentially their own responsibility since they are responsible for their ends. It follows that not only results but also efforts count: hence 'among the criteria for judging the rightness and wrongness of a situation will be included the *striving* to implement positive rights'.[44] On this interpretation as well, the distribution of inputs is vitally important, for this determines what the opportunities really are, but its importance lies not so much in who consumes what, but rather who *could* consume what if he so desired. It is the availability of, or ready access to, facilities (such as schools, water, health care, public transport and so on) rather than the actual level of their utilization, that provides the relevant criterion of evaluation.

3.4 Excellence

In looking for objective criteria of development, some have invoked the notion of excellence. The level of development of a society could on this view be measured by the extent to which excellence is achieved. This is not an approach that comes naturally to economists. The nearest they have come to introducing the principle of excellence into their analyses is their use of the notion of 'merit goods'. These are goods and services, the consumption of which is supposed to carry special merit, above and beyond the call of mere preference. In the case of such goods, even economists with firm free-market convictions agree that it may be socially optimal to produce an output greater than what individual preferences, as expressed by market-signals, would suggest; hence that public expenditure for this purpose is justified. It is accordingly in such contexts as public finance or urban planning that the notion of merit goods has been usually invoked.

By a simple generalization, some measure of the consumption of a bundle of merit goods could also be used as a social indicator. However, the discussion of merit goods by economists usually fails to demarcate 'merit' from some other concepts. Thus, the provision of subsidized housing for vulnerable groups (the elderly, the homeless, refugees) has been described as a merit good, but this is justified by need rather than merit. More often the 'merit' principle is subsumed under that of preference. Thus, in a widely used textbook on town and country planning, Willis[45] defines merit goods as 'those economic goods whose consumption is so meritorious they are provided in excess of the rates of consumption chosen by individuals in the market place' (p. 58). He goes on to state two alternative sets of assumptions from which the logic of this definition can be derived. The first is 'that "the public" has poor taste and that an elite possessing some distinguishing characteristic (e.g. greater intelligence, compassion etc.) ought to impose its preferences on it'; the second that because of uncertainty or the lack of information, individuals are unable to make choices 'consistent with their own preferences' (p. 58). The circumstances described by the second assumption confer no merit on the goods as such and, prima facie, could not justify the social provision of anything other than information itself, while the first assumption seems to rest on authoritarianism moderated by wishful thinking. (One suspects that not that many individuals have actually attained elite-hood by virtue of an exceptional level of intelligence and perhaps fewer still by virtue of compassion. Indeed, members of some ruling elites even pride themselves on their *lack* of these qualities.) Logically, on this reading, merit is ascribed not to specific items of consumption or activity, but to certain individuals, groups or classes and as a consequence to their preferences, whatever these may happen to be. Such an approach does not therefore provide a basis for excellence to be regarded as an *independent* criterion for the assessment or appraisal of social states.

While excellence could exist in many different activities, accepting excellence as a criterion of evaluation in its own right normally implies also accepting the activity itself as having some special merit or intrinsic worth. War and religion have generally been accepted from ancient times as such worthy endeavours. Religious wars have in consequence been regarded as particularly worthy, and at least in some parts of the world, they still appear to exercise a powerful appeal. In some societies competitive games have been locked upon as being second in importance only to war, as an appropriate area for the pursuit of excellence by an individual or a nation. Art, music and literature on the other hand tend to be minority interests. The minority who do desire them have always sought to justify the provision of such goods by claims of excellence rather than their own desires. Shelley, for instance, found it 'indisputable that the highest perfection of human society has ever corresponded with the highest dramatic excellence'.[46] Economists, on the other hand, as our comments above on the definition of merit goods suggest, face considerable analytical difficulty in trying to justify special claims to resource allocation for such concerns. Excellence or 'merit' could however be invoked as separate principles of resource allocation as well as of social wellbeing. Social indicators could, in principle, be devised accordingly. Indeed, statistics of this kind are now commonly used, although often in a casual and ad hoc rather than a systematic way, and more in newspapers or popular journals than in academic discussion; examples are trends in numbers of Olympic gold medals or of Nobel prizes won by various countries, whether in the aggregate or on a per capita basis, and in the distribution of papers published in reputed scientific journals according to the residence, nationality or country of origin of authors.

Emphasis on excellence is often accompanied by a disdainful attitude towards claims based on basic needs, human rights or desire fulfilment, and even towards the very notion of a standard of living that is defined in terms of the wellbeing of the masses of the people rather than that of the worthy few. Excellence, it seems, can be achieved only through a commitment to elitism. In Western culture, an abiding influence in favour of this outlook has been Plato's. That women, slaves and 'barbarians' are inferior by nature and, as such, incapable of achieving excellence; that increasing material standards of living for the many is not a worthy goal for a civilized society; that on the contrary true merit belongs to things that can only be pursued by a few, none of these propositions are obviously true and none, one must concede, originated with Plato,[47] but he did a lot to make them intellectually respectable.[48] The argument is pervasive in his writings but perhaps most explicit in the *Georgias*, which has been described as an attack on the way of life of *any* society which measures its wellbeing by the standard of living of its citizens.[49] According to Plato, the great leaders of ancient Athens had in truth been 'no better than pastry-cooks, stuffing the common people with material goods'.[50] It was, he suggests, concerns such as these, rather than the misdeeds of a few politicians, or a particular political party, that had led to the ruin of Athens and the corruption of its music and drama, its society and politics. If a society was to achieve 'true' greatness, its concerns must be fundamentally different. What really mattered was the maintenance of high standards, even though these were of necessity beyond the reach of the masses of the people. His country's first need, 'was not for a new machinery of living but for a new way of life which at least a few might try to follow.'[51] Much of the contemporary anti-growth literature that we referred to in earlier chapters is replete with notions of this kind.

Plato was worried by the spectre of equality, i.e. equality among citizens. Slavery he took for granted. But even some modern scholars have sought to defend that ancient institution by an appeal to the demands of excellence. We can, asserts Vogt, appreciate Greek slavery as an expression of 'vitality' ('which demanded that a man have a complete and active life, even at the expense of others') as well as of 'devotion to spiritual considerations'.[52] He concedes that there is an attendant loss of humanity but this is a necessary price that had to be paid for the Greek achievement.[53] Essentially similar arguments have been advanced in defence of hierarchical systems, such as caste, that have played a crucial role in some other civilizations.

The proposition that excellence required inequality has found favour with some archaeologists as well as with historians. Archaeological evidence, it is said, shows the central role of inequality in the development of cultures. Pre-historic farmers and hunter-farmers, so runs the argument, were severely limited in their development by the egalitarian nature of their societies, suggested by their artefacts and the pattern of their housing settlements. By contrast, hierarchy and social inequality not only accompanied but were the formative factors in the emergence of high cultures. The conclusion is drawn that civilization itself is essentially a celebration of hierarchy and inequality.[54] I find such arguments quite unconvincing. Logically, why inequality should be expected to foster excellence is far from clear. Indeed, an important argument for equality in the sense of equality of opportunity, including in particular the opportunity of education, has always been that it would increase a society's chances of achieving excellence. Whether one thinks of the abolition of feudal privilege and the opening of careers to talent, or on a grander scale, of Marx's argument in favour of socialism that the free development of all was a condition for the free development of each, the argument in its own terms is a powerful one. It fails only if one believes in a natural hierarchy of intrinsic ability, based for example on race or caste, to which actual inequalities in a society always correspond. There is no reason whatsoever for believing this.

There are also certain difficulties both of logic and fact that arise in assessing past events, whether historical or pre-historical. In order to justify the kinds of judgement that we have just described, one needs to know not only what happened but also what could have happened, and this is extraordinarily difficult. Until quite recently production possibilities even in relatively advanced societies were very narrowly circumscribed. This, together with unequal access to the means of production, produced a hierarchical structuring of society. This was true of all societies. Some hierarchical societies did leave behind an impressive record of achievement in various fields. Others did not. Hence, neither the historical nor the archaeological evidence will bear the heavy weight of causal interpretation that has been laid on it.[55] To say that civilization in ancient societies was effectively limited to a few, does not imply that the quality of that civilization was higher the fewer the number to which it was limited. For all we know, lesser inequality might even have helped such societies achieve more!

My final point, which concerns the present and the future rather than the past, is more directly relevant. Most people, even though they may have disagreements about the concept of progress (for example whether progress is bound to occur, whether *moral* progress is possible at all and so on) would surely agree that human knowledge has indeed progressed remarkably during the last two centuries and especially in the recent past, and to a lesser extent the ability to translate that knowledge into social practice has improved as well. Human capability, in general, has greatly increased as a consequence.

From such a perspective, it makes little sense to regard excellence as conditional on greater inequality, whatever their relationship may have been in the distant past. There are cogent reasons, related to savings, incentives and the urge to prove oneself, why the existence of *some* degree of inequality may provide a spur to achievement; but I believe that in most contemporary societies the existing degree of inequality is much more than what such considerations would justify. In such conditions less inequality rather than more is likely to contribute to the achievement of excellence. On the other hand, equality cannot guarantee excellence, which may turn not only on the development of capability in general but on the existence of special or extraordinary talent, historical circumstances, the *zeitgeist*, motivation, effort, even luck. What is important is to recognize that some social and economic arrangements may be more conducive to the achievement of excellence than others. Hence a claim based on such achievement may well be appropriate, along with others, in assessing relative social performance, but it should not be allowed to 'hijack' the other claims.

3.5 Some Other Considerations

Some social indicators that have been used in the literature of development economics appear not to be covered by our classification. This could be because their aim is different, i.e. other than to serve as indicators of social wellbeing. Alternatively, while not directly linked to social wellbeing themselves, they may stand for something else which contributes to social wellbeing on grounds of desire, need, right or intrinsic merit. Adelman and Morris' influential work on the inter-relationship between social, political and economic development is a case in point. What they sought to find was 'adequate indicators of institutional traits of nations'[56] and what kind of changes in such traits are most conducive to economic growth for countries at various stages of development. Hence, they tried to include in their measures 'the most important aspects of economic, social and political institutions and performance' (p. 15). More specifically, they write, 'the social variables were chosen to portray the principal social aspects of urbanization and industrialization; the political indicators were selected to represent leading characteristics of the emergence of modern states; and the economic indices were designed to summarize the changes in economic structure and institutions typical of industrialization and economic growth' (p. 15). Thus they are concerned with identifying 'road blocks' in the process of modern economic growth itself rather than with the question of increases in social wellbeing that this might help achieve. The list of variables used by them,[57] includes only one (namely extent of literacy) that is of direct 'welfare' significance from the point of view adopted in the present study.

Indirectly, however, modernization itself may be valued because it is widely desired by individuals in developing countries; because it helps create a society where, unlike in traditional societies, there may be some hope in the long run of satisfying basic needs of the masses of the people, as well as some individual rights; because it is judged to be of intrinsic merit, not requiring any further justification and so on. In all these respects using indices of modernization as social indicators raises essentially the same issues and can be defended by the same kind of arguments that are involved in the use of other items of collective consumption for this purpose. Defence is an obvious example. It has sometimes been said that using indicators of this kind is unjustified; imputing individual utilities to such goods often seems far-fetched, while convincing reasons for favouring them on moral grounds may be hard to find. The elite of a country, suggests Little, and it is clear from the context that he has developing countries in mind, may hold in esteem objectives that cannot plausibly be inserted into individual utility functions:

We may call these national objectives. They include the desire to be militarily powerful, to be able to exercise influence on international relations to be independent and maybe nonaligned. They include accoutrements that some think are necessary for a proper nation, a conference center, some luxury hotels and a national airline.[58]

Such objectives of development are apparently more likely to be pursued by leaders of developing countries who 'seem to take a more collective, more nationalist view of development than do most Western liberals' (p. 11). Little attributes this to political reasons, others to the 'fact' that while the Western tradition is based on the individualistic 'Judaeo–Christian' ethic, that of Asian and African nations extols the collective.[59] I shall make two comments on this attitude, which is quite common among Western 'liberal' development economists.

First, the question of the welfare significance of 'national objectives' has little to do with any pecularities of developing countries of today. It was pointed out in the previous chapter that the development of economics itself was tied up with the idea of a standard of living. The wealth of a nation consists of the consumption enjoyed by its members. Welfare is related to this consumption. Such an approach necessarily implies a switch away from the nationalist goals that had once been accepted as proper by the Mercantilist School. Even Adam Smith's somewhat extravagant description of defence as being more important than opulence does not ascribe an absolute value to the nation-state; there is no necessary implication either that State, Nation or 'King and Country' constitute additional sources of individual wellbeing or that such entities themselves may be described as enjoying levels of wellbeing. Rather, it can be regarded as a component (unfortunately often the predominant component) of what economists now describe as 'collective consumption', i.e. that of goods which are such that they cannot be split up and sold to some individual buyers while others are excluded from consuming them.[60]

Expenditure on defence, like that on policing, is justified by the consideration of safety for individuals concerned. Hence, ultimately, it is the principle of individual utility that still applies.[61] However, collective goods, by definition, do not easily lend themselves to resource allocation by means of the market. In consequence, decisions about the 'optimum' level of their output are normally made by government. Nevertheless, interpreting 'defence' in this way is far from satisfactory, for 'defensive' and 'offensive' expenditure may not be distinguishable, even in principle; 'defence' is often valued on grounds that have nothing to do with individual utility. For this reason, Smith may justly be accused of having left a gaping hole in his argument, which in the period since has allowed military and collectivist objectives an honourable and sometimes triumphant entry, usually accompanied by much cheering from Western 'liberals'.

To suggest that Western leaders' concepts of development have been, or are, less 'nationalistic' than those of their Asian counterparts is absurd. Western nationalism developed in the course of several centuries of long and bloody wars, in Europe and abroad, and many a colonial war was fought not so much for the benefits to be gained by acquiring the colony but simply to keep out a rival power. National development and empire building were regarded as going together. Such attitudes were not confined to political leaders. They were widely shared by the public at large and sometimes defended with theoretical reasoning by eminent social scientists. Max Weber, who has been described as the founder of sociology, asserted as a matter of principle that the interest of the nation-state was the only legitimate yardstick for social and economic policy and claimed, in particular, that the German national interest required not so much an increase in output as the preservation of the ethnic landscape.[62] A core of such sentiment persists to this day, and policies such as those on immigration[63] and on levels of 'defence' expenditure, are strongly influenced by it. By contrast, nationalism in the Third World is still weak, fragile, underdeveloped, with neither a firm basis in prevalent religious or cultural ethics nor the powerful stimulus of racism that sustained the rise of nationalism in Europe; it is always in danger of being over-run by stronger loyalties; those of tribe, caste, language, religion or community. Little's assertion that leaders of developing countries take a more nationalist view of development 'than Western liberals' could still be true, provided the term 'liberals' is defined narrowly enough (to include only 'true' liberals who are *not* so nationalistic), but in that case the assertion would be a trivial one.

Even though Little over-states the strength of nationalism in developing countries, his observation about the 'accoutrements' frequently found in developing countries is accurate. No regular traveller to capital cities of developing countries in recent years could possibly fail to notice the proliferation of 'five-star' hotels and similar 'amenities' that Little writes about; careful scrutiny would also show both that such facilities were usually built in blatant violation of existing town-planning regulations and that the rate of utilization of such facilities once built was low. The explanation however, could be different from that which Little suggests. As we have seen, one of Adam Smith's principal objections to the extensive regulation of economic activities by the State was that in effect it might serve the private interests of powerful monopolistic groups. This is probably what has happened. Further, some at least of the amenities in question (including hotels in particular) do *not* belong to the category of collective consumption at all; they are excludable in supply and involve rivalness in consumption. Their proliferation has really little to do with collectivist or nationalist objectives, nor perhaps does it have *practical* significance for the construction of social indicators. No one has suggested that the per capita availability of such amenities be used as an index of the standard of living in developing countries.

Justifications of the massive levels of defence expenditure in developing countries almost always appeal to some version of Adam Smith's argument. From this perspective, the acquisition of military strength by a developing country is seen as essentially defensive in intent, as a means of reducing the risk of being attacked, or at least of being subjected to political and economic pressures, while political independence and the ability to carry out autonomous economic policies are themselves regarded as valuable on much the same grounds as those mentioned above in connection with modernization. The problem of identifying the defensive component still remains however.

Whatever the circumstances, to include measures of military strength in an index of social wellbeing would be quite absurd, whether for developed or for developing countries. First, if it *is* an effective instrument for carrying out beneficial policies, looking directly at the effects of policies on the people at large in terms of the fulfilment of needs, rights and desires appears to be much more sensible. Secondly, military strength is essentially a *relative* concept. ('Whatever happens we have got the Maxim gun, or Star Wars, and they have not'.) If countries A and B are rivals, doubling or halving the military strength of each would in effect leave the strength of each unchanged. Increasing *absolute* military strength is therefore an 'instrument' whose effects on national security are, at best, uncertain. At worst, it can lead to spiralling of expenditure on 'defence' in both countries, so that neither external security nor the satisfaction of basic needs can be achieved.

Further, the pursuit of military strength can bring substantial material benefit or an increase in influence and power to social, political or occupational groups, the military establishment, armament manufacturers, the Defence Ministry, a xenophobic political party or a populist President or Prime Minister. 'The Free World/the Motherland is in danger' is a more persuasive slogan than 'More Hotels'! Such groups or persons therefore tend to develop a vested interest in preventing effective peaceful instruments for the achievement of external security from being chosen. Hence, to suppose that expenditure on 'defence' is valued merely as a device for making individuals more secure could be dangerously naive; some devices are clearly designed to make them *less* secure.[64]

I shall conclude this section by commenting on a more basic issue, namely the status of the nation-state itself in the study of economic welfare. Although economists have long abandoned concepts of national welfare that are not based solely on the welfare of individuals concerned, they still appear to believe that a study of welfare levels of the world's population or a segment of it, can only proceed by first partitioning the relevant individuals into those belonging to different States. The State, in other words, continues to be taken as the relevant unit of aggregation. The present study belongs to the same tradition; its major concern is with issues that arise in comparing levels of wellbeing of different national groups of individuals or the same national group at different times. Such a pre-occupation is quite understandable, for the nation-state is a central feature of the modern world. For one thing, policies adopted by national governments crucially affect welfare levels of individuals, for better or worse. For another, relevant data for sub-national groups are often just not recorded. Nevertheless, conceptually, this is by no means the only relevant approach. I shall mention two other approaches that are no less legitimate. One is to consider groups other than national. Feminists claim, for instance, that women's welfare should be studied as such, and some aspects of this are touched on in subsequent chapters. The other, more radical, option would be to regard the whole of humankind as the aggregate. An outcome should then be judged by its consequences for *all*. This is the direction which Wicksell had hoped economic analysis would take.[65] The fact that people are members of national (and other) groups could be a relevant source of information in such a framework as well, but it would not have any fundamental analytical significance. However, such an approach is not yet part of standard economic analysis.

4

Application to
Some Specific Indicators

When they did not know the decimal value of π
Their teachers asked them: Why
Did you not stay in the gutter you came from
But that they did know.

Bertolt Brecht, *Poems*

Oh excellent, I love long life better than *figs*
William Shakespeare, *Antony and Cleopatra*

Among the most widely used indicators of levels of living are the literacy rate among the adult population and demographic indices such as the expectation of life at birth. I shall use both of these in the next chapter. In the present chapter, I shall discuss justification for these two types of indicator and try to answer some objections that have been made against them, especially as applied to the developing countries. The literacy rate will be discussed in the first section and demographic indices in the second.

4.1 Literacy

Perhaps the most common argument used to justify the use of literacy as a social indicator is the supposed link between literacy and economic growth. This justification is of the 'instrumental' kind. A developed industrial society based on modern, factory-based industrial technology, is said to require mass liveracy. However, this is far from being obvious. Ordinary low-level factory work does not directly require literacy. It is the lack of such a requirement which is emphasized in recent studies of trends in literacy during the early phase of the Industrial Revolution. Schofield, for example, found no improvement in male literacy in England during 1750–1815 and cast doubts 'on the utility of positing universal relationships between literacy and economic growth'.[1] Sanderson points out that during 1813–39, not only were workers in the spinning and weaving trades on which the economy of Lancashire depended predominantly illiterate, their literacy levels were also *below* the average for the country, and what is even more striking, the industrial economy which was emerging created a whole range of new occupations requiring *less* literacy than the old ones.[2] The (predominantly female) power-loom weavers for example, had a literacy level less than one-third that of the male hand-loom weavers they replaced. For textile workers taken together, literacy was halved between 1754–84 and 1784–1814, and it declined significantly for metal and transport workers. For males in a wide range of occupations, literacy not only did *not* become more essential as a cultural skill, 'many of the new industrial occupations recruited a mainly illiterate work-force'.[3]

While clearly the advent of the Industrial Revolution neither required[4] nor promoted literacy in England, this experience need not be *generally* valid, for several other considerations could be relevant. For example, it has been suggested that illiteracy could be a greater handicap *now* than in the technologically simpler environment of the first Industrial Revolution. However, in many developing countries industrial technology, except in some specific areas, is *not* particularly complex. Indeed, some developing countries, such as India, have deliberately sought to encourage increases in production in some industries at least, on the basis of even less mechanized techniques than prevailed in eighteenth-century England. Again, the apparent irrelevance of literacy could be a characteristic peculiar to the cotton textile industry in which the operations are such that they can be performed just (or almost) as well by illiterate labour. There may be something in this argument: the development of the cotton textile industry in Russia in the late nineteenth century on the basis of British technology and almost entirely illiterate labour is a case in point. But as noted, the decline of literacy, or its failure to rise, was a general phenomenon in early industrialization in England (and elsewhere).

Unlike the general run of unskilled workers, many of those at higher echelons of the work force – skilled workers and mechanics, supervisors and foremen, book-keepers, accountants and clerks – did, and do, need to be literate in order to do their job properly, and with industrialization, the number of such jobs increased both absolutely and relatively to the size of the total work force. Further, to ensure a regular flow of sufficient numbers of people into such jobs, and their effective functioning, a 'critical minimum' degree of literacy among the general population would be required as well, but mass literacy is not required.

The importance of literacy for modern economic growth appears to have been considerably exaggerated in the literature of development economics. Educationists and social historians, unlike economists, have usually emphasized the 'social' rather than the 'economic' role of education. The 'social investment' aspect of literacy as distinct from its direct 'productive investment' aspect has more to do with attitudes than with knowledge. Factories involve a new kind of work which is repetitive, based on strict discipline and a rigid time schedule, and which requires constant attention and obedience to rules and to authority, attitudes which do not come easily to people used to the very different rhythms of pre-industrial society. To develop such attitudes came to be regarded as an essential part of the process leading to mass literacy. The historical circumstances in which this view became established have been carefully documented by Stone, who points out: 'Putting little children to work at school for very long hours at very dull subjects was seen as a positive virtue, for it made them habituated, if not naturalized to Labour and Fatigue.'[5]

The effect of education on the growth of industrial capitalism was therefore to muster support for the penal and disciplinary aspects of school, which were seen largely as 'conditioning' the child to routinized labour in the factory. Accordingly, order and regularity, punctuality, discipline and obedience came to be regarded as even more important goals of elementary education than knowledge of the three R's. In other countries, the factory did not, perhaps, cast quite such a long shadow on school education. In France, for example, elementary education appears not to have been tied in any obvious way to the demands of an emergent industrial economy; it was always a step behind industrial development, which was itself slow. Nevertheless, the presence of social objectives was real enough, which explains the frequency with which such goals as 'moral training', 'order and submissiveness' or 'respectable behaviour and order in the countryside' are mentioned as the objectives of education in contemporary official and unofficial reports on elementary education in rural France in the eighteenth and nineteenth centuries, a period in which the extent of literacy greatly increased.[6]

That objectives of this kind continue to be important is shown by such studies as Beeby,[7] which mentions 'habits of tidiness, industry, love of country and attitude of respect for authority' as basic goals of education in the developing countries of today. Some empirical evidence on the association between economic growth and improvements in literacy in the developing countries will be considered (from a somewhat different point of view) in our next chapter.

However, as pointed out in the previous chapter, the instrumental view involves a logical difficulty. If literacy is regarded primarily as a means, however efficient, for achieving something else, it cannot then be regarded as a basic need. Thus, if one values literacy because it helps maintain discipline in factories, it is, in effect, factory discipline that one is attributing value to. Conceivably, 'discipline' could be regarded as an excellent thing, with intrinsic merit, and an index of it could be used as a social indicator. An increase in literacy could then be regarded as one of the policies that could help achieve higher values of this index, along with other possible ones such as improvements in managerial practices, profit-sharing schemes, more effective penalties and rewards for performance, a greater sense of belonging on the part of the working class and so on. On such a reckoning, literacy no longer counts as a social indicator in its own right. The same is true if instead of valuing literacy for its contribution to factory discipline, we value it for its contribution to tidiness, order, obedience, patriotism and so on.

Literacy and education in general could also be justified by the principle of individual preference, i.e. desire fulfilment. Literacy, on this view, is valued because people desire, or desire their children, to be literate. On this view, which underlies the standard economic analysis of education, the reasons for such a preference are not particularly important. The benefits of education at each level are sought to be measured by the earnings differential that corresponds to relevant sequential increase in this level. The justification of education, and of literacy in particular, is therefore based on exactly the same principle that underlies the use of GNP. The difficulties involved in evaluating education, and especially primary education, in this way are well-known and I shall not try to discuss them here.[8] I should, however, like to touch on a matter raised by Blaug, namely whether one can meaningfully talk about the consumption benefits of education at all, for students may not enjoy the actual process of being educated or acquiring literacy. Thus, according to Blaug,

A large part of what is usually thought of as the consumption component of education is in fact forward-looking, involving the anticipated consumption of the services of a durable consumer good; motivated as it is by utilities that accrue in the future, it is more akin to investment than to consumption. Since this form of consumption benefit of education is almost certainly positive – very few people enjoy life less for being educated – higher lifetime earnings are not the only motives that impel individuals to acquire more education. But the same thing is not necessarily true of the current consumption of education which, for all we know, may actually carry negative utility for the average student.[9]

This account of the matter which appears to interpret utility in terms of a 'felicific' calculus in the spirit of Bentham is unsatisfactory in several respects. There is first of all the problem of defining the specific educational input, the utility of which is being considered. This could be a particular class, a course of lectures, a stage or year of attending school, a degree or diploma and so on. The amount of utility derived, and even possibly its sign, could vary accordingly. Our concern however, is essentially with the utility of being (rather than only of becoming) literate.

The more important point is that in modern economic analysis a preference ordering or a utility function representing such an ordering is normally interpreted in terms of desire fulfilment rather than a balance of pleasures and pains. On this interpretation one may prefer or derive utility from education even if one does not enjoy the educational process. The same may be true of a visit to the dentist. Hence no particular problem need arise in speaking of a want or desire for education, as the passage cited appears to imply.

Using the extent of literacy as an indicator of the level of living of a society could also be justified on the ground that literacy is a basic need, irrespective of whether or not people desire to be literate. To qualify as a basic need, literacy must be deemed to be essential for normal human functioning, in the same way as certain minimum levels of food, clothing, shelter and so on are essential. The argument that it should indeed be regarded in this way rests on the belief that unlike many other skills, those associated with literacy are essential to the development of one's potential as a human being. By contrast, illiteracy is seen as narrowing and restrictive. From this point of view the extent of literacy appears to be a natural and obvious indicator of the quality of life and hence of the level of living.

The view described has itself been supported by at least two different arguments. One, set out by Adam Smith, in what is perhaps the first systematic treatment of the virtues of mass literacy, links literacy to the development of the intellectual faculties. To be illiterate is in effect to be mutilated and deformed in this essential aspect of human nature. Hence, mass illiteracy according to Smith tends to perpetuate 'gross ignorance and stupidity' among the 'inferior ranks of the people' and so to benumb their understanding.[10] Literacy to be sure is not sufficient to reach understanding but it is an essential first step along the path leading to it. It is partly for this reason that Smith favours state intervention to promote elementary education among the masses of the people, even if they may not particularly desire such education.

The other argument emphasizes the centrality of writing to civilization. Civilization, it has been said, could not exist without writing. The reason is that writing created certain possibilities for the storage of information over time and its transmission across space, which were immensely superior in quantity and quality from what was permitted by word of mouth. Illiteracy restricts one's access to this complex legacy: it is for this reason that in medieval Latin the word for 'illiteracy' was 'idiotae'. It is also this that explains the extraordinary importance attached to this kind of skill ever since the invention of writing made it possible.[11]

Literacy has also been justified in terms of rights, but a rights-based justification can itself be of several kinds. Thus, for example, it has been suggested that the value of education is to be measured not only by its utility consequences for a person, '. . . but also by the additional range of relationships he can have with people and things – something one may argue, he has a right to'.[12] Another version of the rights-based approach to education holds that education can be truly regarded as a right only in a society where all individuals enjoy a full range of civil and political liberties: 'Even if elementary education must discipline children, the ultimate purpose of education on a rights theory will be to equip every child with the intellectual means to choose a way of life compatible with the equal freedom of others.'[13] Perhaps more persuasive than these is the view of literacy as an essential 'positive' right; literacy is a right to which individuals are entitled *because* it constitutes a basic need.

I shall now consider some views critical of literacy which have become influential in recent years. The critics, too, hold the 'instrumentalist' view of literacy but, unlike some others who share this view, deplore the ends sought to be achieved by it. Hence, they decry accounts ascribing intrinsic merit to literacy as 'the literacy myth'. Instead, they regard literacy simply as a means devised by capitalist society for exercising control over the working classes. On this view, the interpretations of literacy based on individual preferences, basic needs or rights are untenable. However, it is a superficial view, for the consequences of literacy are far more complex than such 'control theories' suggest. In all societies, for a very long time, it was mass illiteracy rather than mass literacy, which provided a means of social control. Restricting access to literacy exclusively to certain selected occupations, groups or castes proved to be an effective device for maintaining a stable hierarchical structure in ancient societies. Contrariwise, societies where the structure of hierarchy seems to have been, by then prevailing standards, relatively less rigid and participation in processes of social decision making relatively more widespread, were commonly societies with a greater measure of male literacy.[14]

Even in early modern Europe, while some education for the middle ranks of lay society came to be regarded as acceptable, the ruling elites were in general suspicious of and hostile to mass education, even at an elementary level, precisely because this was deemed to be a potential danger to the existing order. The argument commonly advanced against mass education in eighteenth- and early nineteenth-century England was twofold. First, by reading undesirable radical pamphlets people would become seditious and unreligious, a danger both to Church and State; secondly, education would give people ideas above their proper station and make them both unwilling and unfit for manual work. Very similar reasons were given in pre-revolutionary France for opposing mass education, including literacy; unchecked education would wreck farming and trade and it would create more expectations of non-manual jobs than could possibly be satisfied, and by doing so, it would undermine the stability of a society which depended on an individual's unquestioning acceptance of the prospects in life ascribed to him at birth. Some societies have tried to prevent reading by the populace altogether. In eighteenth- and early nineteenth-century America, slaves were legally required to be kept illiterate on the grounds that 'teaching slaves to read and write tends to dis-satisfaction in their minds, and to produce insurrection and rebellion'.[15] Similar reasoning could explain the well-known reluctance of colonial governments to establish village schools (or even to encourage their establishment by others). This in time created the legacy of near-universal illiteracy that so many developing countries inherited at independence.

Interpreting mass literacy merely as a means of social control has another important limitation: it too readily identifies the goals of an educational system with its effects. The 'hidden curriculum' of schools, indeed often their open curriculum as well, invariably includes an element of control. It by no means follows that children attending schools are more likely to become passive, docile and easier to manipulate than those who are not. Indeed, there is much evidence that precisely the contrary might be true. For example, the strong links between the rise of mass literacy and that of working-class radicalism in the countries of Western Europe have often been commented on by historians. In England, by the close of the eighteenth century, i.e. at a fairly early stage of the Industrial Revolution, the most class-conscious and articulate members of the working class seem to have regarded reading not primarily as a means of functioning more effectively in one's workplace, nor even simply as a recreation, but essentially as a way to self-respect and dignity, a mark of the new culture of individual self-improvement. Working-class radicals came to accept reading as 'part of being a rational man, who could exploit fully the opportunities of an industrial society'.[16] It is this that explains their efforts to impart elementary education to their children, first by trying to create an alternative type of informal schools which were less authoritarian and more academic and, from around the mid-nineteenth century, to improve facilities for working-class children within the state educational system. A similar interpretation is also borne out by experience in some Asian countries during the twentieth century. It explains, for example, why campaigns for wiping out illiteracy have been an important part of mass-based anti-colonial and national movements, especially those with Communist leadership.[17]

A somewhat different argument for questioning the merits of literacy rests on the proposition that its effects are wholly culture specific. This can be regarded as a variant of the thesis that literacy is a device for social control of the individual. What it asserts is that the consequences of such control depend entirely on the culture. In some cultures, the social control exercised through literacy enriches the individual; in others, it cannot. On this view, a recent statement of which can be found in Pattison,[18] reading and writing in themselves are merely mechanical skills with no inherent virtue; their effects depend entirely on the wider world view and culture into which these skills are introduced. This argument is used to deprecate efforts at increasing literacy in the developing countries. Literacy, suggests this author, is the legacy of Greece and an intrinsic part of Western culture. In that culture, the diffusion of literacy has indeed served to foster both economic development and individual enlightenment. But this need not be the case in other cultures. Hence, it is argued, the assumption that the spread of literacy in Third World countries would help produce similar economic or spiritual benefits there is mistaken.

Such an argument appears to contradict much concrete evidence that the spread of literacy confers such benefits in all cultures, whether Western or otherwise. Pattison himself refers to a well-known study of the effects of literacy in East Pakistan which concludes that literacy helps broaden mental horizons. It finds, inter alia, that workers who can read and write tend to identify with larger units than those who do not; the villager who reads also sees himself as a citizen, as belonging to a nation and even as a member of the world community. Pattison accepts this finding, which many other studies of the effects of literacy in developing countries have shown as well. What he rejects is the conclusion that such an individual is thereby made more civilized. The man who has learned to read has contact with information that comes from beyond the horizons of his village or tribe, and he might naturally feel himself to be a participant in a larger nexus of events than those to which he had formally been accustomed. But the expansion of horizons does nothing to increase tolerance or wisdom. 'Reading may stimulate the Asian or African to contemplate events beyond his immediate neigh-bourhood, but he is likely to approach these events just as he does those within his more limited native community' (p. 127). Indeed, the increased access to information given their 'traditional' attitudes and standards could, suggests Pattison, lead to *lower* levels of civilization.[19]

Pattison's argument lacks a basis in either fact or logic. Literacy did *not* originate in the West,[20] and more to the point, irrespectively of where literacy had its origin, until quite recently the masses of the people in all countries were illiterate. Logically, Pattison's suggestion that Afro-Asians are culturally incapable of reaping the true benefits of literacy brings out, once again, the racist implications of the cultural–determinist argument.[21] Adam Smith's argument that literacy helps to improve understanding appeals on the contrary to our common humanity.

I shall now consider a criticism of literacy of a less extreme kind. This does not deny the merits of literacy but argues that they have been overstated, for while developing new skills, literacy may also destroy old ones. The net benefits of literacy could therefore be much less than its gross benefits. The loss of oral skills brought about by the spread of literacy is the most commonly cited instance of such a possibility. In a pre-literate society, the oral tradition provides the predominant means of transmitting information from one generation to the next. The information may relate to sacred texts, ethical norms and social behaviour or to specific skills such as cooking and carpentry, and it may be passed on not only through the family and kinship group, but also through religious bodies or the village community as a whole. It is the existence of such channels of communications that has ensured the continuity of traditional knowledge in pre-industrial and pre-literate societies. Such societies, therefore, tend to put a high value on oral skills. With the spread of mass rural literacy this is no longer the case. The consequent loss or deterioration of traditional oral skills may be regarded as a cost of literacy, which has also to be considered in the total reckoning. More generally it has been suggested that the spread of adult literacy in a largely illiterate society tends to have the effect of placing the experience and acquired knowledge of older members of the community at a discount, which could lead to a real social loss.[22]

The value of this argument is in drawing our attention to the fact that even literacy may have hidden opportunity costs. However, these are probably fairly low. For instance, the statement that literacy tends to make experience and acquired knowledge obsolete is contradicted by what actually happened in a country such as Japan, which was successful at a fairly early stage of industrialization in achieving a high degree of adult literacy. Far from being eroded, the respect for experience and acquired knowledge, rather than, say, for birth and status, was established on a much firmer basis than had been possible before.[23] The same is true of the supposed conflict between literacy and the oral tradition.

The advent of mass literacy does *not* mark the end of oral tradition. On the contrary, in all countries where mass literacy has spread, religious texts, epics, ballads and folk tales were among the first things to be recorded in print and sold in cheap editions to large numbers of people. The oral tradition, itself, 'came to be transmitted through the written word'.[24]

Secondly, in all pre-industrial societies, certain segments of the population are in effect excluded from the mainstream oral tradition prevailing in the society concerned, from which their own sub-cultures have long remained entirely isolated. For them the acquisition of basic literacy marks the beginnings, not only of articulateness, but also of at least some limited access to the general body of information available in the society as a whole. These would simply not be possible in the absence of literacy.

Thirdly, even if there are up to a point, some substitutes for literacy, they are hardly efficient or adequate substitutes. Opportunities for the transmission of knowledge that the oral tradition of pre-industrial civilization permits are restricted within fairly narrow limits. They can occur only in direct face to face stiuations, and only old and orthodox techniques can be passed on. For this reason, oral transmission of knowledge across generations can be successful only in stagnant societies in which sons invariably follow their father's occupations by reason of caste or custom, and where there is little technological progress. The possibilities of learning new techniques and skills which are ensured by reading are incomparably greater.

The UNESCO is quite right, therefore, in asserting ' . . . that the objective transformations wrought by any development process cannot come about as long as one is exclusively confined to oral communication; such communication although functional in static contexts, does not allow sufficient accumulation and use of knowledge in changing societies'.[25] It is this fact which is missed by radical critics of 'the literacy myth' who have recently discovered the superior virtues of the oral tradition.[26] Some of them have carried the argument a step further to its logical, if absurd, end, by putting the blame not merely on literacy as such, but on modern society of which it is part. They would rather have the rhythms of pre-industrial society, as well as its oral tradition.

Schooling, argues Verne,[27] may indeed help men to break out of a society in which they are born servants and not masters of their own fate, yet in that society they were farmers or craftsmen, disposing of a fair amount of freedom of choice and control over their own daily lives. 'The sons of farmers or craftsmen, who go to school in order to acquire the right to work in factories or in government offices, will have the opportunity of consuming goods unknown to their parents on the farm or in the village. Yet in so doing, they will be surrendering their control over their time and over the social dimensions of their environment' (p. 287). At this point the argument comes very close to some of the anti-growth and environmentalist positions which figure in our earlier discussion in chapter 1, though Verne perhaps is more consistent in facing up to the consequences of his argument. Thus, for him, individual preferences do not matter. People may be foolish enough to wish to be educated, or as Verne puts it: 'The experience of several poor countries shows that even where the school system is only weakly established, it nonetheless represents an image whose power of attraction is far too strong' (p. 297). Hence, he concludes, it must not be allowed to continue to exist! De-schooling could be achieved by organized political action, for ' . . . the major political fact in the years to come is going to be the recognition of the significance of *and the hopes placed in illiteracy* seen as a cultural expression and a manifestation of a balanced interaction with the environment' (p. 286, italics added). For one inspired by this particular brand of utopia, the concept of literacy as an indicator of levels of living would naturally have little appeal.

4.2 Demographic Indices

Demographic indices, namely those describing the incidence of mortality, have been widely used as indicators of levels of living, and of socio-economic conditions in general. Age-specific death rates, in particular that for infants (age group 0–1) and for children (age group 0–4), as well as the expectation of life at birth, i.e. the number of years that a cohort of a population just born and subject to age-specific mortality rates prevailing now would live on average, are especially informative from this point of view. The crude death rate, because it is highly sensitive to the age composition of the population, is less useful. Economic historians often rely on mortality indices when comparing levels of living across time or space, sometimes perhaps because such data are available while national accounts data are not, but this is not the only reason. Thus, in a classic study, E. P. Thompson remarks:

The controversy as to living standards during the Industrial Revolution has perhaps been of most value when it has passed from the somewhat unreal pursuit of the wage-rates of hypothetical average workers and directed attention to articles of consumption, food, clothing, homes and beyond these, health and mortality.[28]

In the same spirit, Laslett refers to the infant mortality rate as 'that favourite measuring rod of welfare'[29] while, according to Eversley, 'It is probably feasible to write the history of the standard of living in terms of the expectation of life at birth'.[30]

Economists have usually been loth to use demographic indices in this way, though they are perhaps much less so now than in the past. As the profession has become increasingly conscious of the limitations of GNP as an index of welfare, non-monetary, 'physical' indices have acquired greater respectability in economic literature, and among these, both the expectation of life at birth and the infant mortality rate figure fairly prominently.

To economists, individuals' preferences for a longer life would seem to be the natural basis for the use of life expectancy as a social indicator. This also finds support from some analyses by philosophers of the value of prolonging human life.[31] By assigning a central place in their account to the fact that individuals tend to prefer a prolonged life, they too sund a utilitarian note. The interpretation of what precisely is being preferred by individuals varies between different accounts however. The view that is generally expressed in this literature is that an individual's preference for a prolonged life is essentially a preference for experience. The earlier a person dies the less experience he has. While this view of the matter corresponds to common sense, it needs clarification in two important respects.

First, there is a certain ambiguity in interpreting an individual's preference for prolonged life as a preference for 'experience', for there could be bad experiences (which would lead to a lowering of the individual's utility level) as well as good ones (which would increase it). The experiences which are excluded by death include the bad as well as the good. Why then should 'more experience' represented by a longer life be preferred as such? There are two possible ways out of this difficulty. One is to suppose that what individuals prefer is the possibility of experience rather than experience itself, i.e. they prefer a prolongation of life in the sense of continued existence, whatever that life is like. The other is to regard an individual's preference for a longer life as a preference for expected future experiences. Only because, or to the extent that, the expected future experiences carry a positive utility, can a prolongation of life be said to be justified on the individual preference criterion. It is this second interpretation that appears more appropriate for our purpose. It has two important implications. One is that, unlike the first version, it allows consideration of the quality of life. If the additional experiences which constitute a prolonged life are expected to lead to a marked deterioration in its quality, it is not assumed a priori that the individual necessarily prefers such a prolongation. The bearing of this consideration on the interpretation of recent increases in the expectancy of life at birth in developing societies will be discussed further below.

Defining preference for a longer life in terms of experience, rather than mere existence, also implies that the utility to an individual of the extension of his life by a given period will vary (in general, inversely) with the age at which this extension occurs. This is so for two distinct reasons. One follows from the 'quality of life' argument itself; the incidence of mental and physical deterioration, and consequent decline in the quality of life, increases sharply beyond a certain age. The other reason is that the experiences resulting from a prolongation of life will depend on one's plans, projects and activities which may be related to one's age. As Brock[32] observes: 'Prolonging life ten years for a person at age 50 who can then complete and carry out the projects, plans and commitments that have shaped her life may be vastly more important or valuable to that person than extending her life an additional 10 years at the age of 80 when the extended projects and commitments of her life plan are essentially completed, even assuming no significant physical or mental deterioration'. The conclusion may not always be quite so clear-cut.

Not only does the age at which significant decline in the quality of life is brought about by physiological factors vary greatly between individuals, it has also been increasing over time as a result of advances in medical knowledge. And projects, plans or activities that an older person can profitably carry out depend in part on prevailing social arrangements which could themselves change as people tend to live longer. The increase in the age of retirement that has occurred in some countries experiencing a marked increase in life expectancy is an obvious instance of such change. Nevertheless, the insight yielded by Brock's argument, namely that an increase in the average life span resulting predominantly from a reduction in deaths in early age or in the prime of life, is more worthy of acclaim than an equal increase brought about by reduction in deaths among the elderly is, I think, valid and I shall return to this point in chapter 5.

Secondly, as our discussion above already implies, the increased experience that a prolonged life gives one *includes* increased consumption of goods and services but is not identical with this; it includes a great many other things as well. Individuals' preference for prolonged life is naturally interpreted in the broad sense, as defined over alternative experience streams, not simply over alternative consumption (or earnings) streams. Complex non-economic as well as economic variables are involved and a single monetary index representing over-all valuation seems more than usually difficult to achieve.

Attempts at providing an over-all valuation of prolonging life in monetary terms have, nevertheless, been made by some economists. Such attempts have usually been made for the purpose of evaluating projects which include saving lives/causing death among their benefits/costs.[33] The same approach has been used for example by Usher[34] to impute a monetary value to increase in life expectancy and hence derive an adjusted rate of economic growth which adds up the growth of life expectancy and that of GNP. The results of such an exercise would enable social indicators to be used in a much more rigorous and comprehensive way than we have attempted in this study. The conceptual basis of the exercise remains dubious, however. Apart from problems already noted, we have the following difficulty. The principle of valuing a change underlying these attempts is compensation, i.e. the sum of money which the loser by a change would regard as sufficient to keep him just as well off as he would be without the change. But dead men cannot be compensated. To circumvent this difficulty, those seeking to estimate the 'value of life' have tried to represent probabilities of living longer, rather than living longer itself, as the elements over which individual preferences are defined. In this formulation, mortality rates themselves are included as the arguments of a utility function. But intuitively it seems dubious that a formulation in terms of probabilities (i.e. relative frequencies) of events could eliminate difficulties that have to do with the nature of the events themselves, and Broome[35] has formally shown that if an attempt is made to fix a monetary value on life, it is simply wrong to do so on the basis of people's evaluations of *probabilities* of death.

Attempts to quantify life-expectancy gains in monetary terms suffer from yet another limitation; they take account only of self-interested preferences. Preferences based on concern for others are necessarily excluded, even the concern of parents for children. In the developing countries, the major source of observed gains in life expectancy at birth has usually been the decline in infant mortality. The increase in utility this brings their parents should in principle count as a reason for regarding the change as an improvement in the level of living of the society concerned. On the other hand, Usher's analysis assumes that society places a high value on children's lives *solely* because children themselves ' . . . put high values on their own lives, because they expect to live a long time' (p. 252), an assumption which he concedes is 'implausible'. The role of the assumption of self-interested preferences in economic analysis was discussed extensively in chapter 1. Here, I should like only to observe that while in some contexts the assumption in question is perfectly legitimate, the valuation of life does *not* belong to this category. If life is viewed as experience, that experience may well be affected in a crucial way by 'externalities'. Hence, 'cardinal' valuation of prolonging life in terms of a monetary unit may be unsatisfactory even as a first approximation.

While the use of demographic variables as social indicators has a long tradition behind it, in recent years it has been attacked by some historians who claim that while the decline of mortality did indeed represent an improvement in levels of living in the past, it does not do so any longer. According to them, while a fall in infant and child mortality rates in European countries in the last century was due to higher standards of living, their sharp fall in developing countries in recent years is explained entirely or predominantly by improved medical techniques, introduced from abroad, by a mechanism exogenous to the process of socio-economic development itself.[36] Similar reservations have been expressed about the contemporary relevance of life expectancy. Though widely held, such a view is mistaken.

One of the reasons advanced by Habakkuk[37] for regarding life expectancy gains in developing countries as 'exogenous' to their development is that they are the result of imported technology. These gains, it is argued, are due not to economic development as such but merely to successful programmes of disease control, whether preventative or curative. Such programmes in turn are dependent on imports of drugs, equipment and know-how from abroad which reflect, at any time, the state-of-the-art in the country of origin. Accordingly, so goes the argument, what an increase in life expectancy in developing countries reveals is simply the rate of technical progress in the developed world. Another strand in the Habakkuk argument has received less attention. Although, he said, the relative importance of public health measures in bringing about mortality decline, as compared to that of improved income and consumption, has been higher in developing countries in the recent period than in European countries in the past, even in Europe, economic influences on mortality were probably much less important than public health measures. The difference is that in Europe, public health measures and the improvement in medical knowledge on which they were based, were themselves ' . . . the product of the social and intellectual tradition of the society'.[38] It is not so in the developing countries of today. This raises doubts about the viability of the process of mortality decline in such countries.

How one reacts to such arguments will depend on one's views about the relationship between technology and culture which was discussed earlier. By way of recapitulation, I shall make three brief remarks. First, for an increase in life expectancy to serve as an acceptable criterion of improved levels of living it is not required that the increase be sui generis, which indeed it can never be; borrowing from the past and from other societies and cultures is the normal and often the only way in which a human group can try to achieve viable and sustained progress.

Secondly, successful borrowing is nevertheless far from automatic. To develop effective health and medical care facilites in a country where a large part of the population is poor, illiterate and rural is not simply a matter of placing an import order for improved health: it is a complex and difficult task of social and economic organization. If some countries have more success than others in achieving it, the differences will be duly recorded by demographic indices. There is no justification for rejecting this record on a priori grounds as spurious or uninteresting.

Lastly, borrowing of technology is not peculiar to the health and medical care sectors. Developing countries, both past and present, have borrowed no less for producing food, clothing, electricity and steel. If the use of imported technology makes life-expectancy gains 'exogenous', the same label should be applied to the growth of GNP itself!

Closely linked to the 'foreign origin' argument is the idea that gains in life expectancy in developing countries, which reflect a decline in mortality, are quite unrelated to an improvement in their economic conditions. It has been said that saving lives may even make matters worse.

Until fairly recently people did not achieve a higher life expectation until this was earned, as it were, through better food, more healthful living conditions and an economy able to carry more people. Now the very fact that people are kept alive so easily makes it more difficult to realise these other goals.[39]

Hence, it is argued, increases in life expectancy can no longer be taken as denoting that levels of living have improved in a relevant sense.

Statements of this kind must rest ultimately on some version of the 'quality of life' argument. What they suggest is that although the length of life in developing countries may have increased in recent years, its quality has declined. Our discussion earlier in this section shows that the use of life expectancy as an indicator of the level of living may then, no longer be appropriate. The argument when interpreted in this way does not appear to me to be convincing. It errs in the first instance by failing to distinguish between temporary and long-run effects. A situation of the kind envisaged here can only be a short-period phenomenon, it cannot last. A deterioration of living conditions brought about as a direct result of declining mortality and hence greater numbers, would in the long run bring the decline in mortality to a stop, and a new (neo–Malthusian) equilibrium would ensue.

Eversley is one of the few writers who seem to have grasped the importance of the length of the time horizon envisaged for the point at issue.

Merely to save lives without also at least maintaining food intake and the provision of other necessaries cannot in the long run mean increasing the expectation of life, it would merely lead to the bunching of mortality in the next acute crisis.[40]

Indeed, something like this appears actually to have happened in some low-income countries during the 1970s:because of their failure to bring about a substantial improvement in socio-economic conditions, the rate of fall in mortality experienced earlier slowed down, and in a few cases, the mortality rate may even have increased.[41] This does not show that demographic indices have ceased to be relevant, rather the contrary. Even if a 'turning point' in mortality decline is explained primarily by improvements in medical technology, a sustained fall, especially in the mortality of infants, is seldom possible without accompanying improvements, for example in sanitation, housing conditions and food, and hence in effect, in the quality of life.

Secondly, assertions that extensions of the length of life in developing countries are unrelated to any improvement in the quality of life in such countries as reflected in their socio-economic conditions also err in interpreting 'socio-economic conditions' too narrowly, namely as that which is measured by national income statistics. Usually such assertions are supported by the argument that in many developing countries mortality has declined and life expectancy increased by much more than the rise in real per capita income would lead us to expect. This is taken as showing that changes in demographic indices and those in socio-economic conditions are unrelated. But while measured increase in per capita consumption may be a fairly accurate indicator as far as private, especially marketed, goods and services are concerned, it is probably much less successful in representing certain other types of change that are especially important for mortality decline. Hence, such an approach is unsatisfactory. A number of statistical studies of the decline in mortality in developing countries are now available.[42] These show that the decline was achieved largely by improvements in quality and increases in supply of public goods, notably water supply, environmental sanitation and other public health measures for the prevention and control of communicable diseases; by better training of midwives and higher standards of personal hygiene in rural areas; and to some extent also by improved nutrition and greater regularity in the supply of food resulting from improved storage, transport, marketing and administration. Many of these improvements tend to be poorly reflected in GNP statistics, but such things are surely part of what one would wish to include in the quality of life.

Summing up, this critique of the relevance of life expectancy as a social indicator is misplaced. To regard increased life expectancy simply as a gift of the Magi, the wise men from the West, is to take a view of the demographic process that is much too naive. And as regards the quality of life, a sustained raise in the average duration of life in a society is almost invariably accompanied by an improvement of the conditions in which life in that society is lived. It is where the life of man is poor, nasty and brutish that it also tends to be short. Nevertheless, when applying the life-expectancy criterion in order to compare different social states, it is right and proper to take some of the points raised by the critics into account. Thus, for instance, if we are concerned with changes in life expectancy over time, the period involved should be reasonably long, and highly abnormal years (on account, say, of flood, famine or civil war) should not be taken either as an initial or a terminal year in the comparison. Care should also be taken when interpreting results to draw on available information directly bearing on the quality of life. Indicators of the satisfaction of basic needs, both individually (calorie consumption, water supply, housing, literacy) and as an aggregate (various poverty indices), are especially relevant for this purpose.

5
An Empirical Analysis

One nation can and should learn from another.

Karl Marx, *Grundrisse*

In the previous two chapters, I have discussed at length arguments by which the use of a social indicator to indicate the level of wellbeing of a society or group could be justified. This chapter seeks to provide an empirical analysis; its aim is to apply some of the more acceptable indicators which figure prominently in our earlier discussion, such as the literacy rate and the expectation of life at birth, in order to compare current levels of living in a number of developing countires. It will also examine the pattern of differences among such countries in respect of the degree to which levels of living have improved since the 1960s. Both in comparing levels of living and in comparing changes in these levels, particular attention will be paid to the question of how far comparisons made in terms of the social indicators chosen lead to the same conclusions as those based on per capita GNP. The chapter is organized as follows. Section 5.1 sets out the basic data, which are then used to analyse comparative levels of living in some developing countries. The extent to which levels of living in these countries improved during 1960-82 is discussed in the next section. The third section looks briefly at changes in levels of living which occurred in some European countries during the Industrial Revolution. The final section consists of a few concluding remarks.

5.1 Comparisons of Levels of Living in Some Developing Countries

The basic data which this section will seek to analyse are provided in table 5.1. In addition to GNP per head, other indicators included in this table are the percentage of the population free of poverty, the expectation of life at birth and the adult literacy rate. The data on the last three indicators mentioned refer to three different years – 1975, 1980 and 1982. To facilitate comparison between results based on these and those based on the income measure, corresponding figures for per capita GNP are also provided. The latter are given in colums (3), (5) and (7) respectively of the table and represent per capita GNP converted from the national currency into US dollars at the going exchange rate as computed by the World Bank and reported in the relevant issue of the *World Development Report*. The limitations of this procedure are well-known. Relative prices differ substantially between countries.

The effects of this on the standard of living cannot really be captured by conversion of GNP at the official exchange rate. A distorted picture of comparative 'real' incomes per head is the usual result. It is to correct such distortions that the Kravis adjustment to GNP was designed.[1] That I have *not* used such Kravis-adjusted figures as the basis of the inter-country comparisons made in this chapter, is due simply to the fact that this would have meant excluding a number of countries, including China, for which the Kravis adjustment factor is not available, and which I wished to include. A number of comparisons between the rank orderings of countries by Kravis-adjusted per capita GNP and by other criteria were also carried out, though the results are not reported in this study. It was found that the conclusions reached in this chapter are *not* affected thereby. This is not really surprising, for while the Kravis adjustment materially affects the magnitude of the per capita GNP figures and hence that of the differences in per capita GNP between rich and poor countries (differences tend to be smaller when the Kravis adjustment is used), it has little effect on the *rank ordering* of countries by per capita GNP, on which we shall concentrate.

TABLE 5.1   *Levels of living in selected developing countries*

(1)	(2)	(3)	(4)	(5)	(6)	(7)	(8)
			% of				*Life*
		GNP per	*Population*	*GNP per*	*Adult*		*expectancy*
	Population	*head in*	*above*	*head in*	*literacy*	*GNP per*	*at birth*
	in millions	*US $,*	*poverty line,*	*US $*	*rate (%),*	*head US $in years*	
Country	*1982*	*1975*	*1975*	*1980*	*1980*	*1982*	*1982*
Bangladesh	92.9	72	40	130	26	140	44
Ethiopia	32.9	81	38	140	15	140	48
Nepal	15.4	n.a.	n.a.	140	19	170	47
Burma	34.9	88	44	170	65.9	190	55
Zaire	30.7	105	51	220	54.5	190	55
Uganda	13.5	115	55	300	52.3	230	47
India	717.0	102	54	240	36.2	260	55
Tanzania	19.8	118	54	280	79.0	280	52
China	1,008.2	n.a.	n.a.	290	65.5	310	67
Sri Lanka	15.2	185	90	270	86.1	320	69
Ghana	12.2	255	81	420	30.2	360	55
Pakistan	87.1	121	66	300	26.2	380	50
Kenya	18.1	168	52	420	47.1	390	57
Afghanistan	16.8	n.a.	n.a.	—	20.0	390	57
Sudan	20.2	112	53	410	32.0	440	47
Indonesia	152.6	90	38	430	57.3	580	53
Egypt	44.3	238	86	580	38.2	690	57
Thailand	48.5	237	77	670	88.0	790	63
Philippines	50.7	182	71	690	75.0	820	64
Nigeria	90.6	176	73	1,010	34.0	860	50
Morocco	20.3	266	84	900	28.0	870	52
Peru	17.4	503	85	930	80.0	1,310	58
Turkey	46.5	379	89	1,470	68.8	1,370	63
Colombia	27.0	352	86	1,180	81.0	1,460	64
Malaysia	14.5	471	92	1,620	60.0	1,860	67
South Korea	39.3	325	94	1,520	93.0	1,910	67

Sources: As indicated in the text

The other indicators are shown in columns (4), (6) and (8) of table 5.1. Column (4) gives the percentages of the population *not* living in poverty, as estimated by Aluwalia Carter, Chenery and Development Policy Staff.[2] Essentially these represent the percentages of the population with sufficient income to satisfy their basic needs of calories. Column (6), which gives the adult literacy rate, i.e. the proportion of the population aged 15 and

TABLE 5.2 *Rank orderings of selected developing countries by GNP per head and by the proportion of population above the poverty line*

(1)	(2)	(3)	(4)
Country	Rank by GNO per head, 1975	Rank by proportion of population above poverty line, 1975	(3) − (2)
Bangladesh	1	3	+2
Ethiopia	2	$1\frac{1}{2}$	$-\frac{1}{2}$
Burma	3	4	+1
Indonesia	4	$1\frac{1}{2}$	$-2\frac{1}{2}$
India	5	$8\frac{1}{2}$	$+3\frac{1}{2}$
Ziare	6	5	−1
Sudan	7	7	0
Uganda	8	10	+2
Tanzania	9	$8\frac{1}{2}$	$-\frac{1}{2}$
Pakistan	10	11	+1
Kenya	11	6	−5
Nigeria	12	13	+1
Philippines	13	12	−1
Sri Lanka	14	21	+7
Thailand	15	14	−1
Egypt	16	$18\frac{1}{2}$	$+2\frac{1}{2}$
Ghana	17	15	−2
Morocco	18	16	−2
South Korea	19	17	−2
Colombia	20	$18\frac{1}{2}$	$-1\frac{1}{2}$
Turkey	21	20	−1
Malaysia	22	22	0
Peru	23	23	0

Source: Computed from data of table 5.1

over who are deemed to be literate, uses statistics from two different sources, namely the *Statistical Year-Books* published by *UNESCO* and the Social Data Sheet of the World Bank.[3] Column (8) reports figures on the expectation of life at birth in years, as given in the World Development Reports, or in a few cases, in national-level demographic studies.

As regards the choice of countries to be included in the

TABLE 5.3   *Rank orderings of selected developing countries by GNP per head and by life expectancy, 1982*

(1)	(2)	(3)	(4)
Country	Rank by GNP per head in US $, 1982	Rank of life expectancy, 1982	(3) − (2)
Bangladesh	1½	2	+½
Ethiopia	1½	6	+4½
Nepal	3	4	+1
Burma	4½	14	+9½
Zaire	4½	8	+3½
Uganda	6	4	−2
india	7	14	+7
Tanzania	8	10½	+2½
China	9	24	+15
Sri Lanka	10	26	+16
Ghana	11	14	+3
Pakistan	12	8	−4
Kenya	13½	16½	+3
Afghanistan	13½	1	−12½
Sudan	15	4	−11
Indonesia	16	12	−4
Egypt	17	16½	−½
Thailand	18	19½	+1½
Philippines	19	21½	+2½
Nigeria	20	8	−12
Morocco	21	10½	−10½
Peru	22	18	−4
Turkey	23	19½	−3½
Colombia	24	21½	−2½
Malaysia	25	24	−1
South Korea	26	24	−2

Source: Computed from data of table 5.1

comparison, this is bound to be arbitrary in some degree. I have included all countries which are (a) usually regarded as developing countries, (b) which had a population of at least 10 million people in 1982 and (c) which had a GNP per head of less than US $ 2000 at the official exchange rate in 1982. These criteria could be disputed but the reader can check that adding

TABLE 5.4   *Rank orderings of selected development countries by GNP per head and by adult literacy rate, 1980*

(1)	*(2)*	*(3)*	*(4)*
Country	*Rank by GNP per head in US $, 1980*	*Rank by adult literacy rate, 1980*	*(3) − (2)*
Bangladesh	1	3	+2
Ethiopia	2½	1	−1½
Nepal	2½	2	−1½
Burma	4	17	+13
Zaire	5	13	+8
India	6	9	+3
Sri Lanka	7	23	+16
Tanzania	8	20	+12
China	9	16	+7
Pakistan	10½	4	−6½
Uganda	10½	12	−1½
Sudan	12	7	−5
Kenya	13½	11	−2½
Ghana	13½	6	−7½
Indonesia	15	14	−1
Egypt	16	10	−6
Thailand	17	24	+7
Philippines	18	19	+1
Morocco	19	5	−14
Peru	20	21	+1
Nigeria	21	8	−13
Colombia	22	22	0
Turkey	23	18	−5
South Korea	24	25	+1
Malaysia	25	15	−10

Source: Computed from data of table 5.1

some of the smaller or richer countries to this list does not materially affect our results. It may also be noted that the countries included in our list account for over three-quarters of all individuals living in developing countries.[4]

The question how far GNP per head points in the same direction as other indicators may be sought to be answered in

TABLE 5.5 *Rank orderings of selected developing countries by GNP per head and by child/infant mortality rates, 1982*

(1)	(2)	(3)	(4)	(5)	(6)	(7)	(8)
Country	Infant mortality rate, 1982	Child mortality rate, 1982	Reverse rank by (2)	Reverse rank by (3)	Rank by GNP per head, 1982	(4) − (6)	(5) − (6)
Bangladesh	133	19	3	9	1½	+1½	+7½
Ethiopia	122	25	5	2	1½	+3½	+½
Nepal	145	22	2	5	3	−1	+2
Burma	96	12	14	16	4½	+9½	+11½
Zaire	106	20	10	7½	4½	+5½	+3
Uganda	120	22	7	5	6	+1	−1
India	94	11	15	17	7	+8	+10
Tanzania	98	18	13	10	8	+5	+2
China	67	7	20	20	9	+11	+11
Sri Lanka	32	3	24½	24	10	+14½	+14
Ghana	86	15	16	12	11	+5	+1
Pakistan	121	17	6	11	12	−6	−1
Kenya	77	13	19	14½	13½	+5½	+1
Afghanistan	205	35	1	1	13½	−12½	−12½
Sudan	119	23	8	3	15	−7	−12
Indonesia	102	13	12	14½	16	−4	−1½
Egypt	104	14	11	13	17	−6	−4
Thailand	51	4	22½	22	18	+4½	+4
Philippines	51	4	22½	22	19	+3½	+3
Nigeria	109	20	9	7½	20	−11	−12½
Morocco	125	22	4	5	21	−17	−16
Peru	83	8	17½	19	22	−4½	−3
Turkey	83	9	17½	18	23	−5½	−5
Colombia	54	4	21	22	24	−3	−2
Malaysia	29	2	26	25½	25	+1	+½
South Korea	32	2	24½	25½	26	−1½	−½

Sources: United Nations, *Demographic Yearbook, 1982*, New York, 1983, and table 5.3

different ways. One way, which is currently popular, is to apply multiple regression analysis to the data so as to test the degree of dependence of one characteristic on others. But this imputes 'cardinal' significance to the figures which may be rather more than they can really bear. Alternatively, one could use measures which only use the ordinal property of indicators. Such an approach is followed in tables 5.2–5.5 which set out the rank orderings of countries according to the various indices. Because not all the indicators are available for all the countries, the list of countries included in each table is not the same. Each rank ordering is in ascending order of magnitude of the indicator concerned. For instance in table 5.2, column (2), Bangladesh is assigned the rank 1 by GNP per head while Malaysia has the rank 25. This means that of the 25 countries on this list, Bangladesh has the lowest GNP per head and Malaysia the highest. Similarly [table 5.4 column (3)], Ethiopia has the lowest adult literacy rate, South Korea the highest, while [table 5.2, column (3)] Peru has the highest proportion of its population above the poverty line, i.e. the lowest poverty ratio. Again that India has the rank 6 in terms of GNP per head in 1980 [table 5.4, column (2)], is equivalent to saying that there are five pair-wise comparisons among these countries by GNP per head in which India comes out as the 'winner', i.e. in which India has a higher value of this indicator.

When two or more countries happen to have the same value for an indicator, the total of the ranks available for distribution is divided equally among them. Each of the countries concerned then has an equal, 'tied' rank. Thus [table 5.4, column (2)], Ethiopia and Nepal have the same GNP per head, which is higher than that of only Bangladesh, with rank 1. Hence, each of the two countries is given a rank equal to half the available rank sum available for distribution, i.e. half of 2+3=5. Much of the discussion in this section will focus on the indicators set out in table 5.1. Data on two others, namely the infant mortality rate (i.e. the death rate per 1000 under 1 year of age) and the child mortality rate (i.e. the death rate per 1000 for the age group 1 to 4 years), both of which are usually regarded as powerful influences on life expectancy at birth, and the resulting rank orders, are also shown in table 5.5. These rank orders, especially that based on infant mortality, were found to be very similar to those based on life expectancy, as expected.[5]

A standard measure of the strength of association when observations are only given an ordinal significance is Spearman's coefficient of rank correlation. The values of this coefficient between per capita GNP and other indicators were calculated for the data of tables 5.2–5.5 and are reported in table 5.6.

TABLE 5.6   *Spearman's rank correlation (ϱ)*
between GNP per head and other indicators

	ϱ
Percentage of population above poverty line	0.94
Life expectancy at birth	0.60
Adult literacy rate	0.46
Infant mortality rate (reverse rank)	0.58
Child mortality rate (reverse rank)	0.54

The rank correlation coefficient between GNP per head and each of the other indicators considered in table 5.6 turns out to be statistically significant.[6] Among these, the strength of association of GNP per head is strongest with the proportion of population above the poverty line and weakest with the adult literacy rate, while its association with the demographic variables stands in between. In the light of the discussion in previous chapters, these results are not, perhaps, particularly surprising. Further remarks on their significance are made in subsequent sections of this chapter.

The rank correlation coefficient measures the overall strength of association between any two characteristics. Even if this association is strong, an individual country could come out much better relatively to other countries by one characteristic than by another. Information of this kind is set out in tables 5.2–5.4, in each of which column (4) shows for each country the result of subtracting its rank as given in column (2) from that in column (3). These figures can be interpreted in the following way. For any country, a *positive* figure in column (4) indicates that its level of living relative to others is assessed more favourably by the indicator represented in column (3) than that in column (2). A negative figure indicates that the opposite is true. If the figure is zero, this shows that assessment according to the two indicators is identical. Thus, in column (4) of table 5.4 the rank–difference figure for Sri Lanka is +16, that for Morocco is −14. This tells us that Sri Lanka's level of living as expressed by adult literacy is a great deal better than what is indicated by its per capita GNP, while in the case of Morocco, it is a great deal worse. I shall now consider some possible explanations of large differences existing between a country's ranking by per capita GNP and its ranking by another indicator.

A country's per capita GNP is simply what each person would have if each had precisely an equal share of GNP. There is of course no such country, nor, perhaps, could there be. However, the extent of inequality in the distribution of income varies from one country to another and such variation could be an important reason for divergence arising between a country's rank order by per capita GNP and that by life expectancy. Life expectancy, it is true, cannot vary between individuals nearly as much as consumption or income. A civil servant in a developing cuntry may well have an average income that is 50 times as much as that of an agricultural labourer, but the expectation of life at birth for civil servants there would not be 50 times as much as that of agricultural labourers! Nevertheless, it would certainly be higher for the former group. Accordingly, if as between two countries with similar levels of per capita income, one had a grossly unequal income distribution while that in the other was more egalitarian, we would expect the former country to come off worse on the life-expectancy criterion.

This hypothesis cannot be easily tested, for statistics of inequality indices for developing countries are still scarce, while figures for inter-group or inter-class differences in life expectancy within a country hardly exist at all. Some idea of whether the hypothesis has any merit may however be had by comparing table 5.3 with the data in table 5.7 on inequality, expressed as the income share of the lowest quintile. That this provides only a partial and limited measure of income inequality is not, in the present context, entirely a disadvantage for it is at the lower end of the income distribution that the considerations which concern us here are most likely to arise, if they arise at all.

A comparison of tables 5.3 and 5.7 suggests the following points. First, there are four countries, all with low per capita GNP, showing high positive scores in the last column of table 5.3. These are Sri Lanka (16), China (15), Burma (9½) and India

TABLE 5.7   *Income inequality in some developing countries*

Country	Percentage share in household income of lowest 20 per cent of householders
Peru	2.5
Kenya	2.6
Turkey	2.9
Malaysia	3.5
Colombia	3.5
Sudan	4.0
Morocco	4.0
Nepal	4.6
Egypt	5.1
Philippines	5.2
Thailand	5.6
South Korea	5.7
Tanzania	5.8
Burma	6.5
Indonesia	6.6
China	6.8
Bangladesh	6.9
India	7.0
Sri Lanka	7.3

Sources: *World Development Report*, various issues. The figure for each country refers to the latest available year for which it is available.

(7). According to table 5.7, in each of these countries the degree of income inequality is relatively low, the income shares of the bottom 20 per cent being 7.3 per cent, 6.8 per cent, 6.5 per cent and 7.0 per cent respectively. On the other hand, there are two countries showing high negative scores in table 5.3, Sudan (-11) and Morocco ($-9\frac{1}{2}$), which also appear in table 5.7, each with a high degree of income inequality, the income share of the lowest quintile for each being only 4 per cent. For Nigeria, which has a score of -12 in table 5.3, the figures for quintile income shares are not available, but the Gini coefficient reported for an earlier year was quite high (0.51).[7]

Broadly speaking, the data support the view that divergence between rankings by per capita GNP and by the expectation of life at birth could be partly due to variations in the extent of income inequality. The explanation is far from complete however, and some anomolous cases do remain, for instance Peru and Turkey have extremely high income inequality but neither has a *high* negative score. On the contrary, Indonesia which has a score of −4, has *low* income inequality. Clearly, other factors, historical or climatic ones perhaps, must be involved as well.

Whether differences in the extent of income inequality could also help explain rank-order differences as between per capita GNP and adult literacy is more questionable. In many of the countries listed, elementary schooling is, at least on paper, free as well as compulsory and has been so for quite some time, usually since achieving political independence. If adult illiteracy still persists, this cannot on the face of it be ascribed to income inequality. There are, it is true, opportunity costs of schooling (income foregone) which may keep poor families from sending their children to school and there may be *some* direct costs as well.[8] But probably more important are facts such as a failure to provide enough schools in rural areas, widespread social discrimination against people belonging to particular castes or tribal groups which, in practice, restricts their access to schooling, the reluctance of parents to send female children to school, the absence of effective adult-literacy programmes and so on. Thus, mass illiteracy may simply reflect social backwardness, which persists, increases in per capita GNP notwithstanding. Income inequality may only be involved if and in so far as such societies themselves tend to have a grossly unequal distribution of incomes. A comparison of tables 5.4 and 5.7 may still provide suggestive clues.

Countries such as Sri Lanka, Burma, Tanzania, China or Thailand, which show much higher ranks in literacy than in per capita GNP, tend to have relatively low income inequality, while in those for which the literacy ranks tends to be considerably lower than the rank by per capita GNP, inequality is normally high. A deeper understanding of the problem may perhaps be gained by looking at the social factors directly. These could be especially important for female literacy. Most of the countries showing high negative scores in table 5.3 are countries with a large or predominant Moslem population. In Islamic societies

TABLE 5.8   *Male and female literacy rate, per cent, in selected countries*

Country	(1) Male	(2) Female	(3) (2)/(1)
Afghanistan	33.2	5.8	0.17
Egypt	53.6	22.4	0.42
Indonesia	77.5	57.7	0.74
Malaysia	69.1	46.8	0.68
Morocco	33.6	9.8	0.29
Nigeria	45.6	23.0	0.50
Pakistan	36.0	15.2	0.42
Turkey	83.2	53.4	0.64

Sources: UNESCO, *Statistical Yearbook*, various issues

women are said to have a low status. For this reason, even if literacy is regarded as a good thing for men, the same may not apply to women. Female literacy may be thought, at best, to be unimportant. Some may even be persuaded that it is undesirable, for literacy could have the effect of making women *less* fit for the role they are traditionally expected to perform. If such attitudes are widely shared in the community at large or have a powerful influence on educational policy, low female literacy rates may be expected to persist, irrespective of the rate of economic growth, and for that matter, irrespective of the rate of male literacy. This would tend to depress the overall literacy rate. Some idea of how important in practice such considerations are, may be had from the figures shown in table 5.8 on male and female literacy in some predominantly Moslem countries for the latest year for which such figures were available (which in most cases was 1980).

Taken together these countries also showed a figure for the ratio of female to male literacy that was lower than the corresponding figure for the other developing countries, which provides some prima facie evidence for a cultural connection. In Afghanistan and Morocco, and to a lesser degree in Egypt and Pakistan, the literacy rate for females is not only extremely low, it is also far lower than for the male population. The achievement of widespread female literacy in such countries may well require social, political and cultural change even more than economic growth as such. Yet, contrary to doctrines of cultural determinism, such barriers do not appear to be insuperable. The ratio of female to male literacy varies considerably *among* countries listed in table 5.8, and cultural barriers to female literacy appear to have been crossed much more successfully in some (Turkey, Malaysia, Indonesia) than in others. The process, it is true, is still incomplete. In some of the countries being discussed there exist organized groups fiercely opposed to 'Western' values and committed to the preservation of 'indigenous' culture, of female illiteracy in particular. Increasing overall literacy in such countries or even maintaining its present level, could depend crucially on how far society is able to resist 'radical reactionary' pressures of this kind.

There are a number of other rank-related measures which one could also use.[9] Instead I shall explore an alternative route, the rationale of which may be explained as follows. A statement that a GNP index of wellbeing could point in the wrong direction may be interpreted as meaning that, in a pair-wise comparison, the GNP measure could give a ranking which is the reverse of that given by some other index, believed to be a good indicator of social welfare. Thus for example, if GNP per head is higher in *A* as compared to *B*, but the adult literacy rate is lower, then if and to the extent that literacy is a good indicator, the GNP measure is not. And if life expectancy is lower in *A* as well, one would probably be highly sceptical about regarding the level of living as being higher in *A* on the basis of its high per capita GNP alone. A relevant question, therefore, is how frequently such 'mis-direction' is likely to arise. The data of table 5.1 could be made to yield an answer. Further, countries are not random numbers but entities about which we have much other information.[10] It is surely of some interest to note which particular pair-wise comparisons of our countries do in fact show such mis-matching of indices. For this reason, it may be useful to focus on pair-wise comparisons between *all* pairs of countries involved in respect of every indicator in which we are interested. The result of such an exercise is shown in tables 5.9–5.11.

These results could be interpreted in a number of different ways. One is to treat the relationship between per capita GNP and some other indicator, such as the extent of poverty, as one of

TABLE 5.9 *Association between pair-wise comparisons of selected developing countries by GNP per head and by the poverty ratio, 1975*

(1) Country i	(2) Countries with GNP per head $\geqq$ that of i but poverty ratio $\geqq$ that of i, not both equalities holding simultaneously
Bangladesh	Ethiopia, Indonesia
Ethiopia	Indonesia
Burma	Indonesia
Indonesia	—
India	Zaire, Sudan, Tanzania, Kenya
Zaire	—
Sudan	Kenya
Uganda	Tanzania, Kenya
Tanzania	Kenya
Pakistan	Kenya
Kenya	—
Nigeria	Philippines
Philippines	—
Sri Lanka	Thailand, Ghana, Morocco, Colombia, Turkey, Peru
Thailand	—
Egypt	Ghana, Morocco, Colombia, Peru
Ghana	—
Morocco	—
South Korea	Colombia, Turkey, Malaysia, Peru
Colombia	Peru
Turkey	—
Malaysia	—
Peru	—

Source: Derived from table 5.2

simple association. This indeed is all that the table headings lay claim to. Let us assume, for instance, that the data of table 5.1 (from which tables 5.2–5.4 are derived) do reflect a certain stable underlying association between the GNP per head of a country and the percentage of its population living above the poverty line. We could then use the ranking of any two countries in the sample by one of the two criteria, prevailing at some future date, to draw inferences about their ranking by the other. Thus for

TABLE 5.10   *Association between pair-wise comparisons of selected developing countries by GNP per head and by life expectancy at birth, 1982*

(1)	*(2)*
Country i	*Countries with GNP per head ≧ that of* i *but life expectancy at birth ≦ that of* i, *not both equalities holding simultaneously*
Bangladesh	Afghanistan
Ethiopia	Bangladesh
Nepal	Uganda, Afghanistan, Sudan
Burma	Zaire, Uganda, India, Tanzania, Ghana, Pakistan, Afghanistan, Sudan, Indonesia, Nigeria, Morocco
Zaire	Pakistan, Afghanistan, Sudan, Nigeria
Uganda	Afghanistan, Sudan
India	Tanzania, Ghana, Pakistan, Afghanistan, Sudan, Indonesia, Nigeria, Morocco
Tanzania	Pakistan, Afghanistan, Sudan, Nigeria, Morocco
China	All countries in table 5.3 with GNP per head higher than China except Sri Lanka
Sri Lanka	All countries in table 5.3 with GNP per head higher than Sri Lanka
Ghana	Pakistan, Afghanistan, Sudan, Indonesia, Nigeria, Morocco
Pakistan	Afghanistan, Sudan
Kenya	Afghanistan, Sudan, Indonesia, Egypt, Nigeria, Morocco
Afghanistan	—
Sudan	—
Indonesia	Nigeria, Morocco
Egypt	Nigeria, Morocco
Thailand	Nigeria, Morocco, Peru, Turkey
Philippines	Nigeria, Morocco, Peru, Turkey
Nigeria	—
Morocco	—
Peru	—
Turkey	—
Colombia	—
Malaysia	South Korea
South Korea	—

Source: Derived from table 5.3

TABLE 5.11 *Association between pair-wise comparisons of selected developing countries by GNP per head, and by adult literacy rate, 1980*

(1)	*(2)*
Country i	Countries with GNP per head $\geq$ of i but adult literacy rate $\leq$ that i, not both equalities holding simultaneously
Bangladesh	Ethiopia, Nepal
Ethiopia	—
Nepal	Ethiopia
Burma	Zaire, India, China, Pakistan, Uganda, Sudan, Kenya, Ghana, Indonesia, Egypt, Morocco, Nigeria, Malaysia
Zaire	India, Pakistan, Uganda, Sudan, Kenya, Ghana, Egypt, Morocco, Nigeria
India	Pakistan, Sudan, Ghana, Morocco, Nigeria
Sri Lanka	All countries in table 5.4 with GNP per head greater than Sri Lanka's except Thailand and South Korea
Tanzania	All countries with GNP per head greater than Tanzania's except Thailand, Peru, Colombia and South Korea
China	Pakistan, Uganda, Sudan, Kenya, Ghana, Indonesia, Egypt, Morocco, Nigeria, Malaysia
Pakistan	—
Uganda	Pakistan, Sudan, Kenya, Ghana, Egypt, Morocco, Nigeria
Sudan	Ghana, Morocco
Kenya	Ghana, Egypt, Morocco, Nigeria
Ghana	Morocco
Indonesia	Egypt, Morocco, Nigeria
Egypt	Morocco, Nigeria
Thailand	Philippines, Morocco, Peru, Nigeria, Colombia, Turkey, Malaysia
Philippines	Morocco, Nigeria, Turkey, Malaysia
Morocco	—
Peru	Nigeria, Turkey, Malaysia
Nigeria	—
Colombia	Turkey
Turkey	—
South Korea	—
Malaysia	—

Source: Derived from table 5.4

example, if it is known at that time that country *A* has a higher extent of poverty, one could use the former ranking as a surrogate for the latter; country *A* would be regarded as having a lower proportion of its population above the poverty line. Table 5.9 could then be used to estimate the 'probability' of such a prediction being wrong. Thus, according to this table, the relative frequency of a false prediction of the kind described is the number of 'mis-matched' pairs divided by the total number of pairs, that is 30 divided by the number of combinations of 23 things taken two at a time. This relative frequency equals 0.12 approximately and can be regarded as an estimate of the relevant probability.

A similar interpretation holds when the GNP per head is matched with life expectancy at birth (table 5.10), or with the adult literacy rate (table 5.11). Rather than asking how often GNP per head orders country pairs differently as compared to some other indicator, one could look at how often GNP per head gives the 'wrong' orderings as compared to those given by *each* of two or more such indicators. Thus, for each country *i*, one could identify which countires, if any, have GNP per head greater than or equal to that of *i*, but for which any two, or all three, of the other indicators considered in tables 5.9–5.11 respectively – namely the proportion of the population above the poverty line, life expectancy at birth and the adult literacy rate, are less than or equal to that of *i* (not all equality signs holding simultaneously). The probability of a 'mis-match' of each type is shown in table 5.12. Alternatively one could add a dash of causality to the analysis.

According to standard economic doctrine, discussed in chapter 1, the direction of causality is from GNP per head to the level of poverty. The higher the per capita GNP, the lower should in the long run be the incidence of poverty, hence the higher the percentage of the population enjoying levels of living above the poverty line. On this reading, what table 5.9 shows is that the impact of income on the level of poverty is indeed very strong, but it is not inevitable. There is a sizeable body of exceptions, to the tune of 12 per cent, where higher GNP per capita fails to reduce poverty. Such cases clearly call for special investigation; the distribution of assets and of income among classes and

TABLE 5.12   *Probability of higher GNP per head being a wrong predictor for other indicators in pair-wise comparison*

Other indicator	Probability
(1) Proportion of population above poverty line	0.12
(2) Life expectancy at birth	0.29
(3) Adult literacy rate	0.34
(4) (1) and (2)	0.04
(5) (1) and (3)	0.05
(6) (2) and (3)	0.21
(7) (1), (2) and (3)	0.03

Sources: As described in the text

households might require special attention; one would wish to know whether poverty is concentrated in certain regions or ethnic groups, and so on.

These remarks have brought us close to yet another interpretation in which GNP per head is regarded only as a means of achieving some other objective. If the desired objective can be achieved at a lower level of GNP per head, this would, on this interpretation, be regarded as a cost-efficient outcome. Thus table 5.9, column (2), lists, for each country the countries j for which per capita GNP either exceeds or equals that of i, as does the poverty ratio, subject to the qualification that not both equalities hold at the same time. On the interpretation now being considered, the number of such countries can be given an evaluative significance. The higher the number against a given country, the more efficient it is relative to others in respect of the poverty indicator. The table could thus be used to establish an efficiency raking among the countries with respect to the objective of reducing poverty. And similarly for the other indicators considered.

One could also use an alternative definition of 'mis-matching' of pair-wise orderings as between GNP per head and say the poverty ratio. This would start by identifying, for a country i, each country j such that j has a lower, or equal, poverty ratio as compared to *i* (or equivalently, a higher, or equal, proportion of the population that is poverty free), but also has a GNP per head lower than or equal to *i*, with the usual proviso that not both equalities hold simultaneously. The probability of 'mis-match', so defined, could be calculated accordingly, but the interpretation would now be different. Considering, as before, the hypothesis that it is higher GNP per head that causes poverty to decline, the calculations now tell us that a reduction in poverty is indeed *normally* accompanied by an increase in GNP per head but this is not *always* the case. The 'probability' that in pair-wise comparisons a country with lower poverty is one with higher GNP per head turns out to be about 89 per cent, but in the remaining 11 per cent of cases, poverty is lower *without* per capita GNP being higher. Again, the exceptions merit study. They could be ascribed to egalitarian values, an especially favourable initial distribution of incomes, the vigorous pursuit of anti-poverty programmes and so on. To conclude, according to my results while a strictly deterministic interpretation of the relationship between GNP per head and other level-of-living indicators is unconvincing, the view that they are unrelated is absurd.

5.2 Comparisons of Changes in Levels of Living in Some Developing Countries During 1960–1982

So far, I have been concerned with problems that arise in comparing levels of living at a given time. In this section, I shall discuss problems involved in comparing changes in the levels over a period. The period chosen is 1960–82, which is as recent a period as I could get data for and hopefully long enough for change to occur.

I shall begin by considering how changes in indicators could appropriately be measured. It is clear first of all that comparing changes in levels puts a greater burden on the statistics than comparing levels, for assuming (some) 'cardinal' properties of the level indicators can now no longer be avoided. For per capita GNP, the percentage growth rate per year over the period, after correction for price change, provides the obvious indicator of the extent of change. Some possible ways of calculating the extent of change in literacy and in life expectancy at birth are considered below.

The extent of an increase in literacy could be measured in a number of different ways. Suppose, for instance, that over a certain period, the adult literacy rate has gone up from 40 to 80 per cent. The change may be represented as an increase of 40 percentage points: 40 per cent *more* of the population are literate than was the case before. The increase is still measured relative to the size of the population, but it is absolute in the sense that the amount of the increase is *not* measured relative to the initial level of literacy. If this latter approach is followed we get a measure of *relative* percentage increase in literacy, which is in this instance 100 per cent, i.e. the literacy rate has doubled over the period concerned. Yet another way of measuring the change would be to look at the relative decline in illiteracy rather than the relative increase in literacy. In the instance cited, this relative decline is two-thirds, i.e. approximately 67 per cent, from 60 per cent to 20 per cent. Each of these three ways of measuring the same change can be interpreted in a perfectly natural way for the purpose of comparative evaluation of different countries in respect of literacy, but the resulting evaluations may well differ! None of the three is necessarily the best in *all* possible circumstances but the following observations may be relevant in choosing between them. Using the 'increase in percentage points' measure in evaluating a country's performance implies that a gain of a given number of percentage points is to be valued equally, irrespective of the initial literacy rate, for example a rise in the literacy rate from 40 to 80 per cent should count as being of equal merit to a rise from 10 to 50 or from 60 to 100 per cent. If the evaluation function is concave, an equal 'absolute' increase would be regarded as being of greater value the lower the initial level, hence a relative measure, i.e. one based on a percentage change, rather than on a percentage points change, would be more appropriate. But one still has the choice of using an index of the percentage decline in illiteracy or one of the percentage rise in literacy. It is easily seen that the initial level makes a crucial difference to the measurement. If two countries are starting from the same initial level of literacy rate (hence also the same illiteracy rate) per cent, it does not matter which of the two indices we use. One will necessarily rank the two countries in exactly the same way as the other. But this will not be so if the initial literacy rates are different. In that case, given an equal percentage points increment in literacy, a comparison in terms of the relative decline in illiteracy will favour the country with the higher initial level of literacy; that based on the relative increase in the literacy rate has a 'bias' of the reverse kind. If a country is already in a situation of high literacy, the two indices would lead to very different assessments of a country's performance in respect of literacy. Thus if literacy goes up from 90 to 100 per cent, the relative increase in the literacy rate is only 11 per cent but the relative decline in illiteracy is 100 per cent!

Very similar problems arise in measuring the extent of an increase in the expectation of life at birth. The increase can be measured 'absolutely'; an increase in life expectancy at birth from 40 to 50 years would then be described as an increase of 10 years. Alternatively, it can be measured as a relative percentage change, which in this case is 25 per cent. Choosing between the two involves exactly the same considerations as choosing between the 'increase in percentage points' and 'the relative percentage increase' measures of an increase in literacy.

An increase in life expectancy could also be measured in terms of the percentage decline in 'longevity shortfall', i.e. in the number of years by which the expectation of life at birth falls short of a postulated norm. This would correspond to measuring gains in the literacy level by the percentage decline in illiteracy. The 'norm' implicit in that calculation is that all adult persons should be literate. However, I have some reservations about using the same approach in the context of measuring gains in life expectancy. First, for reasons stated in the previous chapter, it is, I believe, appropriate to regard universal literacy as indeed a norm. This justifies the use of measuring the rate of fall in the distance from such a state as an indicator of performance. However, there is no such natural norm in the case of the length of life. One could of course use the prevailing expectation of life in developed countries as an aspiration level, or the maximum achieved by any of the countries in our 'sample' could be used instead. The authority of the Bible could be invoked in favour of 'three score years and ten' as the optimum length of life. Sample surveys could be undertaken in developing countries to ascertain how long people would wish to live; and so on. None of these appear to be satisfactory.

Moral arguments for regarding an extension of the length of life beyond those typically prevalent in the developing countries today as an appropriate indicator of social wellbeing have been stated earlier. But they do not warrant the conclusion that an indefinite extension of the length of life is necessarily to be regarded as desirable, nor that a distance function from a 'correct' life-span provides an appropriate 'metric' for measuring relative advances in life expectancy achieved by different societies. The statistical argument against the 'longevity shortfall' measure is this: if over a given period country *A* achieved an absolute increase in life expectancy exactly equal to that achieved by *B*, but *A*'s initial life expectancy had been higher, the longevity shortfall measure, irrespective of the norm from which shortfall is measured, would necessarily show a sharper decline for, i.e. a better performance by *A*. I do not find this an attractive property.

None of these measures of performance is entirely satisfactory. Essentially, the problem is one of deciding in what way initial conditions should be allowed to influence the index of performance. The choice of an index which determines which country will be deemed to have performed better, is not simply a matter of statistics. It involves both moral judgements and empirical beliefs concerning the nature of the development process. If it is the initial breakthrough from stagnation that one regards as the crucial step in development, one type of index will be preferred. Someone who believes that development is easy to start with but becomes more difficult and worthy of acclaim at its later stages, will incline towards a different type of index.

In practice, judgements about comparative performance by different countires in terms of a given indicator may be less problematic than this discussion suggests. The basic statistics on improvements in adult literacy in a number of countries together with the values of the three indices described are given in table 5.13, while data and indices relating to life expectancy are provided in table 5.14. I shall discuss these in turn.

In view of my remarks on the index number problem, it may

TABLE 5.13 *Increase in adult literacy in selected developing countries, 1960–1980*

(1)	(2)	(3)	(4)	(5)	(6)
Country	Adult literacy rate 1960	Adult literacy rate 1982	(3) − (2) Increase in Adult literacy in percentage points	Relative percentage increase in adult liberacy	Relative percentage decline in adult illiteracy
Afghanistan	8	20	12	150.0	13.0
Nepal	9	19	10	111.1	11.0
Tanzania	10	79	69	690.0	76.7
Sudan	13	32	19	146.2	21.8
Morocco	14	28	14	100.0	16.3
Nigeria	15	34	19	126.7	22.4
Pakistan	15	26	11	73.3	12.9
Kenya	20	47	27	135.0	33.8
Bangladesh	22	26	4	18.1	5.1
Egypt	26	38	12	46.2	16.2
Ghana	27	30	3	11.1	4.1
India	28	36	8	28.6	11.1
Zaire	31	55	24	77.4	34.8
Uganda	35	52	17	48.6	26.2
Turkey	38	69	31	81.6	50.0
Indonesia	39	57	18	46.2	29.5
Malaysia	53	60	7	13.2	14.9
Burma	60	66	6	10.0	15.0
Peru	61	80	19	31.1	48.7
Colombia	63	81	18	28.6	48.6
Thailand	68	88	20	29.4	62.5
South Korea	71	93	22	31.0	75.9
Philippines	72	75	3	4.2	10.7
Sri Lanka	75	86	11	14.7	44.0

Sources: As indicated in the text

be sensible in interpreting table 5.13 to divide our countries into a few broad groups according to the level of literacy prevailing at the beginning of the period. The discussion will focus on differences in the extent of increase in literacy achieved by countries within each group, rather than between pairs of countries belonging to different groups. Let us look first at the countries which by 1960 had already attained fairly high levels of literacy, where a majority of the population of age 15 and over

TABLE 5.14 *Life expectancy in years in selected developing countries,*
1960–1982

	1960	1982	Increase years	Increase (%)	Decline in longevity Shortfall (%)
Bangladesh	42	44	2	4.8	5.9
Ethiopia	36	48	12	33.3	35.3
Nepal	37	47	10	27.0	30.3
Burma	44	55	11	25.0	42.3
Zaire	40	50	10	25.0	33.3
Uganda	44	47	3	6.8	11.5
India	43	55	12	27.9	44.9
Tanzania	42	52	10	23.8	35.7
China	53	67	14	26.4	82.4
Sri Lanka	62	69	7	11.3	87.5
Ghana	40	55	15	37.5	50.0
Pakistan	44	50	6	13.6	23.1
Kenya	47	57	10	21.3	43.5
Afghanistan	34	36	2	5.9	5.6
Sudan	39	47	8	20.5	25.8
Indonesia	41	53	12	29.3	41.4
Egypt	46	57	11	23.9	45.8
Thailand	51	63	12	23.5	63.2
Philippines	51	64	13	25.5	68.4
Nigeria	39	50	11	28.2	35.5
Morocco	47	52	5	10.6	21.7
Peru	48	58	10	20.8	45.5
Turkey	51	63	12	23.5	63.2
Colombia	53	64	11	20.8	64.7
Malaysia	57	67	10	17.5	76.9
South Korea	54	67	13	24.1	81.3

Sources: UN, World Development Report, various issues; longevity shortfall was
computed from a norm of 70 years

were literate. There are eight such countries, ranging from
Malaysia (with an adult literacy rate of 53% in 1960) to Sri
Lanka, for which the corresponding figure was 75%. The other
countries belonging to this category along with their literacy
levels in 1960 are Burma (60%), Peru (61%), Colombia (63%),
Thailand (68%), South Korea (71%) and the Philippines (72%).

Among these, the figures reported in table 5.13 suggest that South Korea, which by 1982 was not far short of achieving the goal of universal literacy, had the most impressive performance of all. It was closely followed by Thailand, Peru and Colombia, among which there was not a great deal of difference in the extent of advance in literacy achieved over the period. Next comes Sri Lanka, which started off the period as the most literate of the lot, but had by 1982 lost its lead to South Korea. Its achievement was far from impressive, but was still considerably better than that of either Burma or Malaysia, both of which performed poorly. Philippines must be reckoned as the poorest performer in this group of countries, whichever of the three indices of literacy gain we choose to adopt.

Let us consider next a group of countries at the lower end of the literacy spectrum, those which in 1960 had literacy levels of less than 20 per cent. There are seven such countries, of which Afghanistan had the lowest level of literacy (8%) in 1960 and Pakistan and Nigeria jointly the highest (15%). The others are Nepal, Tanzania, Sudan and Morocco. One country in this group, Tanzania, had remarkable success; a rise in adult literacy from 10% to 79%. Some have attributed this to a more liberal definition of literacy, but such a change can only have accounted for a small part of the increase. Essentially, mass literacy was achieved by a concentrated and well-planned effort over a relatively short period during the late 1970s. None of the other countries in this group can be compared even remotely with Tanzania. Indeed, the other countries in the group seem to have done pretty poorly, even though, because of the extremely low levels of literacy at the beginning of the period, figures for the *relative* (percentage) rise in literacy tend to be fairly high. We are left with the 'intermediate' group of countries, which had literacy rates in 1960 ranging from 29 to 50 per cent. Of these, Turkey (which raised its literacy level from 38 to 69 per cent) and Kenya (for which the corresponding figures were 20 and 47) may reasonably be said to have performed fairly well. Zaire and Uganda come next. Compared to these, Egypt's performance was distinctly poor, and India's poorer still. At the bottom of the pile come Bangladesh and Ghana, which show little progress. Group-wise rank orders of our countries by each of the three

TABLE 5.15   *Within-group rank orders of developing countries by increase in adult literacy, 1960–1980*

(1)	*(2)*	*(3)*	*(4)*
Country	Rank by increase in adult literacy in percentage points	Rank by relative percentage increase in adult literacy	Rank by relative percentage decline in adult illiteracy
Afghanistan	3	6	3
Nepal	1	3	1
Tanzania	7	7	7
Sudan	5½	5	5
Morocco	4	2	4
Nigeria	5½	4	6
Pakistan	2	1	2
Kenya	8	9	7
Bangladesh	2	2	2
Egypt	5	4½	4
Ghana	1	1	1
India	3½	3	3
Zaire	7	7	8
Uganda	6	6	5
Turkey	9	8	9
Indonesia	3½	4½	6
Malaysia	3	3	2
Burma	2	2	3
Peru	6	8	6
Colombia	5	5	5
Thailand	7	6	7
South Korea	8	7	8
Philippines	1	1	1
Sri Lanka	4	4	4

Source: Table 5.13

measures of an increase in literacy described above are set out in table 5.15.

Our analysis of recent changes in literacy in developing countries is necessarily somewhat perfunctory. A deeper understanding of what has been happening would require close scrutiny of varying concepts of literacy and of the nature of the data on which our analysis is based.[11] More important, it would require examination of the influences which may have helped or hindered the advance of literacy.

Next I shall try to compare countries in respect of their gains in life expectancy. Let us consider the figures reported in table 5.14 in the light of our comments about measurement at the beginning of this section.

There are three countries which 'qualify' as the worst performers in respect of the gain in life expectancy in this period, whether the absolute increase in years or the relative percentage increase is used to measure this gain. There are Bangladesh, Afghanistan and Uganda. Each of the first two recorded an increase of just 2 years in life expectancy and the last of 3 years. These figures are so low even relative to their life expectancy level at the beginning of the period that the relative percentage increase is low as well, being 4.8, 5.9 and 6.8 per cent for Bangladesh, Afghanistan and Uganda respectively. Only slightly better are the performances of Morocco (with an absolute gain in life expectancy of 5 years and a relative gain of 10.6%) and Pakistan (absolute gain 6 years, relative gain 13.6%). Again, at the other end of the spectrum, Ghana comes out clearly as the best performer both in terms of the absolute gain (15 years) and the extent of the relative increase (37.5%). But in between the 'best' and 'worst' performers, the two measures do frequently lead to contradictory rankings. Thus each of the four countries, Nepal, Zaire, Kenya and Peru, show a gain in life expectancy of 10 years, but because they start from different levels, the relative increases achieved are different, being 27%, 25%, 21.3% and 20.8% respectively.

Should Nepal's performance be judged to be just as good as Peru's, as better (on the ground that adding a decade to the average life-span starting from an abysmally low life-span of 37 years deserved to be valued more than the same increase starting from the relatively respectable figure of 48 years) or as worse (on the ground that an increase is harder to achieve, the higher the level one is starting from)? The answer would vary, depending on both the moral and the empirical judgements which we make. If, in addition to the absolute and the relative percentage increase measures of an improvement in life expectancy, we also take into

TABLE 5.16 *Within-group rank orders of developing countries by increase in life expectancy at birth, 1960–1982*

(1) Group	(1) Country	(2) Life expectancy in years, 1960	(3) Increase in life expectancy in years during 1960–82	(4) % increase 1960–82	(5) % decline in longevity shortfall 1960–82	(6) Rank by (3)	(7) Rank by (4)	(7) Rank by (5)
I	Afghanistan	34	2	5.9	5.6	1	1	1
	Ethiopia	36	12	33.0	35.0	5	5	4
	Nepal	37	10	27.0	30.3	3	3	3
	Sudan	39	8	20.5	25.8	2	2	2
	Nigeria	39	11	28.2	35.5	4	4	5
II	Zaire	40	10	25.0	33.3	4½	5	4
	Ghana	40	15	37.5	50.0	9	9	9
	Indonesia	41	12	29.3	41.4	7½	8	6
	Bangladesh	42	2	4.8	5.9	1	1	1
	Tanzania	42	10	23.8	35.7	4½	4	5
	India	43	12	27.9	44.4	7½	7	8
	Uganda	44	3	6.8	11.5	2	2	2
	Burma	44	11	25.0	42.3	6	5½	7
	Pakistan	44	6	13.6	23.1	3	3	3
III	Egypt	46	11	23.9	45.8	4	4	4
	Kenya	47	10	21.3	43.5	2½	3	2
	Morocco	47	5	10.6	21.7	1	1	1
	Peru	48	10	20.8	45.5	2½	2	3

IV							
Philippines	51	13	25.5	68.4	$6\frac{1}{2}$	7	4
Thailand	51	12	23.5	63.2	$4\frac{1}{2}$	$4\frac{1}{2}$	$1\frac{1}{2}$
Turkey	51	12	23.5	63.2	$4\frac{1}{2}$	$4\frac{1}{2}$	$1\frac{1}{2}$
Colombia	53	11	20.8	64.7	3	3	3
China	53	14	26.4	82.4	8	8	7
South Korea	54	13	24.1	81.3	$6\frac{1}{2}$	6	6
Malaysia	57	10	17.5	76.9	2	2	5
Sri Lanka	62	7	11.3	87.5	1	1	8

Source: Table 5.14

account performance as measured by the percentage decline in longevity shortfall, the problem of deciding which country has the better performance becomes quite intractable. Yet all is not lost, for we may at least agree that the initial level does make a difference. Accordingly, it may be useful to concentrate on comparisons among countries starting the period with a similar life expectancy level.

As in the case of literacy, here too it will be useful to divide our countries into several groups according to the initial level of life expectancy. Within each such group, the three types of index of a life expectancy gain described above, namely its absolute increase in years, the relative percentage increase and the relative percentage decline in longevity shortfall, should then be expected to rank performances by different countries in much the same way. This does not of course help in comparing performances of countries belonging to different groups, but from a practical point of view it is differences in performance between countries starting from roughly similar conditions that are probably of greater interest. I have classified the countries into four groups as follows:

Group	Life expectancy in 1960
I	Less than 40 years
II	40–4 years
III	45–50 years
IV	above 50 years

Within each group the various indices of life expectancy gain and the rank ordering of countries by each index are shown in table 5.16. Within-group rank orderings by the three indices of increase in life expectancy used in table 5.16 are, as expected, closely similar. A few exceptions do occur; the ranking of some countries in group IV by the 'percentage decline in longevity shortfall' criterion is very different from their ranking by the other two criteria. Sri Lanka in particular comes out as the best performer in the group according to the decline in longevity-

TABLE 5.17 *Average annual growth rate per cent in real GNP per capita, 1960–1982*

Bangladesh	0.3
Ethiopia	1.4
Nepal	−0.1
Burma	1.3
Zaire	−0.3
Uganda	−1.1
India	1.3
Tanzania	1.9
China	5.0
Sri Lanka	2.6
Ghana	−1.3
Pakistan	2.8
Kenya	2.8
Afghanistan	0.9
Sudan	−0.4
Indonesia	4.2
Egypt	3.6
Thailand	4.5
Philippines	2.8
Nigeria	3.3
Morocco	2.6
Peru	1.0
Turkey	3.4
Colombia	3.1
Malaysia	4.3
South Korea	6.6

Source: World Development Report, 1984

shortfall measure but as the worst according to either the absolute or the percentage increase measures of life-expectancy gain. The source of the discrepancy has already been described; the measurement of life-expectancy gain by a percentage decline in longevity shortfall favours the country with a higher initial level of life expectancy.

The strength of association between the level of per capita GNP and levels of social indicators such as the literacy rate, the expectation of life and so on, was discussed at some length earlier in this chapter. Correspondingly, the question arises to what

TABLE 5.18   *Rank correlation coefficient of growth rate of GNP per head with increase in adult literacy, 1960–1980*

Groups	With increase in adult literacy in percentage points	With relative percentage increase in adult literacy	With relative percentage decline in adult illiteracy
I	−0.15	−0.60	0.00
II	0.39	0.47	0.54
III	0.48	0.17	0.38
All	0.27	−0.03	0.40

Sources: Computed from tables 5.13 and 5.17

extent *changes* in levels of such indicators are associated with *changes* in per capita GNP. In the long run, of course, the two questions cannot admit of different answers. If the changes are correlated in a certain way, the levels resulting from them will be correlated in the same way as well. This need not however hold in the short run, during a specific period. I shall be concerned with the period 1960–82. Were the countries which showed the greatest increases in terms of per capita income also those which showed the greatest improvement in literacy, the expectation of life and so on? I shall consider literacy first, classifying countries into three groups and using all three indices of an increase in literacy, as above. The growth rates of GNP per head at constant prices during 1960–82 are reported in table 5.17. The rank correlation coefficients between the growth rate and the measures of literacy increase for each group as well as for all countries together are given in table 5.18. Countries showing negative growth rate of GNP per head over the period were, however, omitted when deriving these. Similarly, rank correlation coefficients between growth rates of GNP per head and measures of increase in life expectancy at birth are reported in table 5.19, again excluding countries with a negative growth rate of GNP per head over the period.

Summing up, developing countries differed greatly in their economic performance, whether performance is reckoned in terms of the growth rate or of improvements in social indicators,

TABLE 5.19 *Rank correlation coefficient of growth rate of GNP per head with increase in life expectancy in developing countries, 1960–1982*

Group	With absolute increase in life-expectancy in years	With relative % increase in life expectancy	With relative % decline in longevity shortfall
I	0.50	0.50	1.00
II	0.39	0.47	0.07
III	0.65	0.80	0.40
IV	0.58	0.51	0.01
All	0.59	0.32	0.61

Sources: Tables 5.14 and 5.17

the adult literacy rate and life expectancy at birth in particular. However, differences in such indicators were not related to those in the growth rate in any simple or obvious way. As tables 5.18 and 5.19 show, some within-group rank correlation coefficients are even negative.[12] Clearly, the strength of association of the growth rate with an increase in literacy is weaker than with an increase in life expectancy at birth. The fact that the correlation between the growth rate and improvements in the level of living is not particularly strong could be interpreted as favouring an optimistic view of the prospects for developing countries, for a low growth rate need not rule out an improvement in the level of living.[13] It could just as easily be given a pessimistic interpretation, for a high growth rate does not guarantee improved levels of living. The actual outcome would depend on circumstances in the country concerned.

I shall conclude this section by taking note of a problem that can arise in interpreting results of our inter-country comparison of life expectancy. A higher life expectancy, it was observed in chapter 4, may not indicate an improved level of living if accompanied by a lower quality of life. It has also been argued that increases in life expectancy in developing countries since the 1960s were generally accompanied by, and indeed largely due to, improvements in living conditions and hence in the quality of life. However, the argument does not appear quite so decisive if we also take account of the extent to which human rights to civil and political freedom are preserved as an important aspect of the quality of life. Some developing countries with an excellent record of achievement in raising life expectancy, and as well, in spreading literacy and alleviating poverty, have in respect of human rights a record that appears to be badly flawed. Comparisons of levels of living, or of changes in these levels, involving cases of this kind raise difficulties which I shall not however, pursue further in this book.

5.3 Parallels from the Past: the European Experience

The last two sections of this chapter were concerned with certain aspects of economic development in the Third World since 1960. In this section, we shall draw some parallels from past European experience. The Industrial Revolution can hardly be said to have suffered from a lack of scholarly attention but surprisingly little of the literature has sought to explore the relationship between economic growth and levels of living in nineteenth-century Europe in a systematic way.[14] This brief discussion cannot, of course, remedy this lack, but I do hope to provide a few pointers in this direction.

In earlier sections of this chapter we have looked at the relationship between GNP per head and a number of other indicators of the level of living. Among the latter, only demographic variables, for the most part the expectancy of life at birth, will be used in this section; this is due to limitations of data on other indicators and of space. I shall look at the growth of GNP per head and of life expectancy at birth in some European countries in two successive periods, namely 1850–1900 and (for a larger group) 1900–29. But first, a word in justification of choice of periods. As regards the initial year, there was actually little choice: for most European countries, life expectancy data for earlier periods are simply not there. However, our concern here is not primarily with life expectancy by itself but rather with the relationship between economic growth and levels of living in Europe. For this purpose 1850 is not perhaps a bad year to start from. Recent work by economic historians, has, it is true, tended to push the origins of industrial revolution in European countries further back in the past.[15] Britain, the first industrial nation, has long been known as a special case. There, industrial revolution is conventionally dated from the beginning of the second half, or at the latest, of the last quarter, of the eighteenth century. There is now considerable evidence which suggests that even in some countries of continental Europe, modern economic growth started near the beginning, rather than the middle, of the nineteenth century. Nevertheless, the fact, if it is one, that 1850 is rather late in the calendar of European industrialization, does not make our results irrelevant, for by all accounts, the earlier phase of industrial growth did little to improve the standard of living.

Historians, who otherwise differ substantially on the standard of living question, agree that in no country did industrialization bring about a general improvement in living conditions for the masses of the people *before* the mid-nineteenth century.[16] Hence, if a relationship between economic growth and an improvement in levels of living exists at all, it is *after* 1850 that we should be hopeful of finding it. At the other end of the period, I wished to avoid the Depression of the 1930s, during which many of these countries experienced negative economic growth, while the remarkable advance both in per capita GNP and in levels of living generally, achieved by them since the end of the Second World War, is really a different story altogether. This makes 1929 a natural cut-off date.

Rank orderings of as many European countries as the data permit, by GNP per head and by male life expectancy at birth, for 1900 and 1929, are presented in tables 5.20 and 5.21 respectively, and those between GNP per head and the infant mortality rate in tables 5.22 and 5.23. Of these, tables 5.20 and 5.22 are the more important for they describe the state of affairs at the end of the classic phase of modern European economic growth, a phase moreover in which at least some of the benefits of growth should have passed on to the masses. The following aspects of table 5.20 deserve comment.

First, there are a few countries which have a low relative level of GNP per head as well as of life expectancy. Russia, which has the lowest figure on both scores, and consequently a zero rank

TABLE 5.20   *Rank orderings of some European countries by GNP per head and by life expectancy at birth, c.1900*

			Male life expectancy at birth in various periods			
(1)	*(2)*	*(3)*	*(4)*	*(5)*	*(6)*	*(7)*
Country	GNP per head in 1960 US dollars, 1900	Rank	Period	Life expectancy in years	Rank	(6)−(3)
Austria[a]	414	5	1901–5	39.14	3	−2
Belgium	721	13	1900	45.11	8	−5
Bulgaria	260	2	1899–1902	39.99	4	+2
Denmark	633	11	1901–5	52.90	14	+3
Finland	425	6	1901–10	45.33	9	+3
Franch	604	9	1899–1903	45.02	7	−2
Germany	639	12	1901–10	44.82	6	−6
Italy	335	3	1901–11	44.24	5	+2
Netherlands	614	10	1901	47.40	11	+1
Norway	577	8	1901/2–1910/11	54.82	15	+7
Russia	248	1	1896–7	31.40	1	0
Spain	351	4	1900	33.85	2	−2
Sweden	454	7	1898–1902	51.53	13	+6
Switzerland	785	14	1901–10	49.25	12	−2
United Kingdom[b]	881	15	1901	45.40	10	−5

[a] The figure for GNP per head refers to Austria–Hungary, while that for life expectancy to Austria. The life expectancy for Austria–Hungary would be between 39.14 and the corresponding figure reported for Hungary (37.1), but its ranking by life expectancy would remain unchanged if the appropriate correction were made.
[b] The figure for life expectancy refers to England and Wales.
Sources: Paul Bairoch, 'Europe's gross national product, 1800–1975', *Journal of European Economic History*, Fall 1976, table 6, p. 286; United Nations, *Demographic Year Book 1967*, New York, 1968, table 29, pp. 722–36; André Armengaud, 'Population in Europe, 1700–1914', in Carlo M. Cipolla (ed.), *The Fontana Economic History of Europe*, Vol. 3, London and Glasgow, Collins/Fontana, 1973, p. 48; Samuel H. Preston, *Mortality Patterns in National Populations*, New York, Academic Press, 1976, table A.1, p. 84; Nathan Keyfitz and Wilhelm Flieger, *World Population*, Chicago and London, The University of Chicago Press, 1968, pp. 30–7.

TABLE 5.21 *Rank orderings of some European countries by GNP per head and by life expectancy at birth, c.1929*

				Male life expectancy at birth for various periods			
(1)	*(2)*	*(3)*	*(4)*	*(5)*	*(6)*	*(7)*
Country	GNP per head in 1960 US dollars, 1929	Rank	Period	Life expectancy in years	Rank	(6)−(3)
Austria	720	6	1930–3	54.50	6	0
Belgium	1,098	14	1928–32	56.02	8	−6
Bulgaria	306	1	1925–8	45.92	1	0
Denmark	945	9	1926–30	60.90	12	+3
Finland	590	5	1930	53.87	5	0
France	982	10	1929–33	54.85	7	−3
Germany	770	7	1932–4	59.86	11	+4
Hungary	424	2	1930–1	48.27	2	0
Italy	517	4	1930–2	53.76	4	0
Netherlands	1,008	11	1928–32	63.28	15	+4
Norway	1,033	12	1921–40[a]	62.53	14	+2
Spain	455	3	1930	48.38	3	0
Sweden	897	8	1928–32	62.02	13	+5
Switzerland	1,265	15	1929–32	59.17	10	−5
United Kingdom[b]	1,038	13	1930–2	58.74	9	−4

[a] The UN *Demographic Yearbook 1967* reports a figure for the period 1921–2/1930–1 and another for the period 1931–2/1940–1. A simple average of the two figure is used here.
[b] The figure for life expectancy is for England and Wales. Estimates of GNP per head are due to Bairoch, *Europes gross national product, 1800–1975*, table 12, p. 297.
Sources: Life-expectancy data are from Nathan Keyfitz and Wilhelm Flieger, *World Population*, Chicago and London, The University of Chicago Press, 1968, pp. 32–6; and United Nations, *Demographic Year book 1967*, New York, 1968, table 29, pp. 722–36

difference, is the prime example, but there are also others in this group for which the magnitude of the rank difference is small; whether its sign is positive (as for Bulgaria) or negative (e.g. Austria, Spain) does not really matter. These countries remind us in a way of Bangladesh and Nepal in table 5.3.

Secondly, there is a group of countries which stand at the very top of the income table, but which do not do nearly so well in the life-expectancy league, and consequently get large negative

TABLE 5.22 *Rank orderings of some European countries by GNP per head and by the infant mortality rate, 1900*

(1)	*(2)*	*(3)*	*(4)*	*(5)*	*(6)*
Country	*GNP per head in 1960 US $, 1900*	*Rank*	*Infant mortality rate per 1,000 live births*	*Reverse rank*	*(5)−(3)*
Belgium	721	13	172	6	−7
Bulgaria	260	2	132	12	+10
Denmark	633	11	128	13	+2
Finland	425	6	153	10	+4
France	604	9	160	7	−2
Germany	639	12	229	2	−10
Italy	335	4	174	5	+1
Netherlands	614	10	155	8	−2
Norway	577	8	91	15	+7
Romania	275	3	197	4	+1
Russia	248	1	252	1	0
Spain	351	5	204	3	−2
Sweden	454	7	99	14	+7
Switzerland	785	14	150	11	−3
United Kingdom	881	15	154	9	−6

Sources: Bairoch, 'Europe's gross national product, 1800–1975', table 6, p. 286; B.R. Mitchell, *European Historical Statistics 1750–1970*, London and Basingstoke, The Macmillan Press, 1975, table B7, pp. 130–1

scores for the rank difference. Germany, with a rank difference of −6, and Belgium and the United Kingdom each with one of −5, clearly belong to this group.

Thirdly, there are the Scandinavian countries, namely Sweden, Norway and Denmark, which differ substantially in respect of GNP per head, but which have very similar, and high, levels of life expectancy at birth.

All three also have positive figures in column (7); +7 for Norway, +6 for Sweden and +3 for Denmark. A very similar picture emerges from table 5.22. There are a few countries with very low levels of GNP per head which also have very high rates of infant mortality (Russia, Romania, Italy, Spain) and, accordingly, record low figures in column (6). An exception is

TABLE 5.23   *Rank orderings of some European countries by GNP per head and by the infant mortality rate, 1929*

(1)	(2)	(3)	(4)	(5)	(6)
Country	GNP per head in 1960 US $	Rank	Infant mortality rate per 1,000 live births	Reverse rank	(5)−(3)
Belgium	1,098	14	110	6	−8
Bulgaria	306	2	156	2	0
Denmark	945	9	83	10	+1
Finland	590	6	98	8	+2
France	982	10	100	7	−3
Germany	770	7	97	9	+2
Italy	517	5	125	4	−1
Netherlands	1,008	11	59	12½	+1½
Norway	1,033	12	54	14	+2
Romania	331	3	197	1	−2
Russia	293	1	155	3	+2
Spain	455	4	123	5	+1
Sweden	897	8	59	12½	+4½
Switzerland	1,265	15	52	15	0
United Kingdom	1,038	13	74	11	−2

Sources: As in Table 5.22

Bulgaria, which despite having the second lowest GNP per head among the countries listed (higher only than Russia), does much better, relatively speaking, as regards infant mortality, and in consequence shows a rank difference of +10. I suspect that favourable climatic factors could have played a part here, but the figure for infant mortality could also be a serious underestimate. Of greater significance is the fact that the United Kingdom, Belgium and Germany, all early industrializing countries, show high negative scores in the last column (as was also the case in table 5.20). Norway and Sweden on the other hand, have high positive scores as before.

How far had things changed in 1929? A look at column (7) of tables 5.20 and 5.21 shows that Belgium and the United Kingdom continue to have high negative rank difference figures and Sweden a high positive one, while the (positive) score for Denmark remains unchanged. On the other hand the rank-difference score for Norway remains positive, but is now much lower in magnitude while that for the Netherlands is positive and higher. The score for Germany changes from high and negative (−6) to high and positive (+4). The significance of this change will be commented on later in the chapter. One notices also that by and large the magnitude of rank differences has diminished, and there are now quite a few countries, not only those at the bottom of GNP per head ranking, that show a zero or small rank difference. This suggests that the rank correlation coefficient between GNP per head and life expectancy at birth must have increased. Calculations show that this is indeed the case. For 1900 the Spearman rank correlation coefficient between GNP per head and life expectancy at birth was 0.61, while that between GNP per head and the infant mortality rate was only 0.28. The former figure, it may be noted, is almost the same as that calculated for developing countries for 1982 (table 5.6, page 000). The association between GNP per head and infant mortality, on the other hand, was much weaker in Europe, the rank correlation coefficient being less than half that found for developing countries in 1982.

Evidently, in Europe at the turn of the century, higher GNP per head was a very poor indicator of lower infant mortality. By 1929, however, this had ceased to be true. While the coefficient of rank correlation between GNP per head and life expectancy at birth now rose to 0.72, that between GNP per head and infant mortality rose, much more strikingly, from 0.28 to 0.78. This could be explained by the fact that while a marked decline of infant mortality in Europe was essentially a twentieth-century phenomenon [a glance at column (4) of tables 5.22 and 5.23 will help bring this out] with economic development, general mortality had started to fall, and hence life expectancy to rise, much earlier. In present-day developing countries, by contrast, improvements in life expectancy have been much more closely tied to a fall in the infant mortality rate.

A more precise idea of what was going on could perhaps be had by looking directly at *changes* in per capita income and in other indicators that occurred during this period. This we shall now try to do.

Some difficulties that arise in choosing a measure of change in life expectancy were mentioned earlier. Both the absolute increase and the relative percentage increase measures will be used in the following discussion. The analysis will be based on changes in *male* life expectancy, but this is not an expression of sexist bias; none of the conclusions would be affected if data on female life expectancy were used instead. Basic information on economic growth and on life expectancy in some European countries during the second half of the nineteenth century is provided in table 5.24, and, for a larger group of countries for the period 1900–29, in table 5.25. In both periods there was considerable inter-country variation in the growth rate as well as in the increase in life expectancy at birth, hence an attempt at analysing the relationship between them appears feasible. As before, for each period I shall compare the rank orders of the countries by growth rates of GNP per head and by increases in life expectancy. In doing so, for reasons stated earlier, I shall arrange the countries into separate groups such that the initial levels of life expectancy within each group are fairly close. The results are shown in tables 5.26 and 5.27.

Most within-group rank correlation coefficients were found to be small; some of them had negative signs, and taken together they suggest that there was no strong association between the increase in life expectancy at birth and the growth rate of GNP per head in either period. However, since these coefficients are based on very small groups, one could question their interpretative significance. Hence, I also computed the coefficients of rank correlation which result when, in each period, the countries are considered together, without breaking them up into groups. These figures are reported in table 5.28; on the whole they do not show any strong association either.

It would be wrong to take low correlation as showing that economic growth did not contribute to the increase in life expectancy in Europe. In pre-industrial Europe life expectancy had long been both low and stable.[17] Countries like Spain or

continued on p. 166

TABLE 5.24 *Economic growth and increase in life expectancy in some European countries, c. 1850–1900*

(1)	(2)	(3)	(4)	(5)	(6)	(7)	(8)
		Male life expectancy at birth in years		*Male life expectancy at birth in years*	*Absolute increase in male life expectancy at birth in years*	*Relative percentage increase in male life expectancy at birth*	*Percentage annual growth rate of GNP per head 1850–1900*
Country	*Period I*		*Period II*				
Denmark	1850–9	43.10	1901–5	52.90	9.80	22.74	1.83
France	1851	38.54	1899–1903	45.02	6.48	16.81	1.20
Germany	1871–81	35.50	1901–10	44.82	9.32	26.25	1.47
Italy	1881–2	35.20	1901–11	44.24	9.04	25.68	0.38
Netherlands	1850–9	36.40	1900–9	51.00	14.60	40.11	0.72
Norway	1846–53	44.90	1901/2–1910/11	54.82	9.92	22.09	1.00
Sweden	1848–52	41.54	1898–1902	51.53	9.99	24.05	1.54
United Kingdom[a]	1838–54	39.90	1901	45.40	4.89	12.26	1.32

[a] The figure for life expectancy is for England and Wales.
Growth rates of GNP per head: Computed from data of table 6, p. 286, in Bairoch, 'Europe's gross national product 1800–1975.

Sources: Life-expectancy data:

Denmark: W.R. Lee (ed.), *European Demography and Economic Growth*, London, Croom Helm, 1979, Appendix table 2.1, p. 111

France, Sweden: Nathan Keyfitz and Wilhelm Flieger, *World Population*, Chicago and London, The University of Chicago Press, 1968, p. 32–3, 36–7 respectively

Germany: Period I, André Armenguad, 'Population in Europe 1700–1914', in Carlo M. Cipolla (ed.) *The Fontana Economic History of Europe*, Vol. 3, London and Glasgow, Collins/Fontana, 1973, p. 48; Period II, United Nations, *Demographic Yearbook 1967*, New York, 1968, table 29, p. 726

Italy: Period I, Lee, *European Demography and Economic Growth*, Appendix table 5.15, p. 227; Period II, UN *Demographic Yearbook 1967*, table 29, p. 732

Netherlands: Lee, *European Demography and Economic Growth*, Appendix table 6.38, p. 281

Norway: Period I, Michael Drake, *Population and Society in Norway, 1735–1965*, Cambridge, Cambridge University Press, 1969, table 3.5, p. 47; Period II, UN *Demographic Yearbook 1967*, table 29, p. 730

United Kingdom: Period I. Armenguad, 'Population in Europe 1700–1914', p. 48; Period II, Keyfitz and Flieger, *World Population*, pp. 36–7

TABLE 5.25 Economic growth and increase in life expectancy at birth in some European countries, c.1900–1929

(1) Country	(2) Period I	(3) Male life expectancy at birth in years	(4) Period II	(5) Male life expectancy at birth in years	(6) Absolute increase in male life expectancy at birth in years	(7) Relative percentage increase in male life expectancy	(8) Percentage annual growth rate of GNP per head, 1900–29
Austria	1901–5	39.14	1930–3	54.50	15.36	39.24	0.35[a]
Belgium	1900	45.11	1928–32	56.02	10.91	24.19	1.46
Bulgaria	1899–1902	39.99	1925–8	45.92	5.93	14.83	0.56
Denmark	1901–5	52.90	1926–30	60.90	8.00	15.12	1.39
Finland	1901–10	45.33	1930	53.87	8.54	18.84	1.14
France	1899–1903	45.02	1929–33	54.85	9.83	21.83	1.69
Germany	1901–10	44.82	1932–4	59.86	15.04	33.56	0.65
Hungary	1900–1	37.10	1930–1	48.27	11.17	30.11	0.82[a]
Italy	1901–11	44.24	1930–2	53.76	9.52	21.52	1.51
Netherlands	1901–2	47.40	1928–32	63.28	15.88	33.50	1.72

Norway	1901/2–1910/11	54.82	1921–40	62.53	7.71	14.06	2.03
Spain	1900	33.85	1930	48.38	14.53	42.92	0.90
Sweden	1898–1902	51.53	1928–32	62.02	10.49	20.35	2.38
Switzerland	1901–10	49.25	1929–32	59.17	9.92	20.14	1.66
United Kingdom	1901	45.40	1929–32	58.74	13.34	29.38	0.57

[a] The growth rates are for the period 1913–29.

Sources: Data on life-expectancy are from Nathan Keyfitz and Wilhelm Flieger, World Population, Chicago and London, The University of Chicago Press, 1968, pp. 32–6; and United Nations, Demographic Year Book 1967, table 29, pp. 722–36.
Growth Rates of GNP per head were computed from data given in Bairoch, 'Europe's gross national product 1800–1975, table 12, p. 297

TABLE 5.26 *Within-group ranks of some European countries by the increase in life expectancy at birth and by the Growth rate of GNP per head, c.1850–1900*

(1)	(2)	(3)	(4)	(5)	(6)	(7)
		Rank by growth rate of GNP per head, 1850–1900	Rank by absolute increase in male life expectancy	Rank by relative percentage increase in life expectancy	(4) − (3)	(5) − (3)
Group	Country					
I	France	3	1	1	−2	−2
	Germany	4	3	3	−1	−1
	Italy	1	2	2	+1	+1
	Netherlands	2	4	4	+2	+2
II	Denmark	4	2	3	−2	−1
	Norway	1	3	2	+2	+1
	Sweden	3	4	4	+1	+1
	United Kingdom	2	1	1	−1	−1

Source: Computed from figures given in Table 5.29. The increase in life expectancy refers to the increase between periods I and II as defined in table 5.24

TABLE 5.27 Within-group ranks of some European countries by the increase in life expectancy and by the growth rate of GNP per head, c.1900–1929

(1) Group	(2) Country	(3) Rank by Growth rate of GNP per capita, 1900–29	(4) Rank by Growth absolute increase in male life expectancy	(5) Rank by relative percentage increase in male life expectancy	(6) (4) − (3)	(7) (5) − (3)
I	Austria	1	4	3	+3	+2
	Bulgaria	2	1	1	−1	−1
	Hungary	3	2	2	−1	−1
	Spain	4	3	4	−1	0
II	Belgium	4	4	4	0	0
	Finland	3	1	1	−2	−2
	France	6	2	3	−4	−3
	Germany	2	6	7	+4	+5
	Italy	5	3	2	−2	−3
	Netherlands	7	7	6	0	−1
	United Kingdom	1	5	5	+4	+4
III	Norway	3	1	1	−2	−2
	Denmark	1	2	2	+1	+1
	Sweden	4	4	4	0	0
	Switzerland	2	3	3	+1	+1

Source: Computed from figures given in table 5.25. The increase in life expectancy refers to the increase between periods I and II as defined in table 5.25

TABLE 5.28   *Coefficients of rank correlation of the growth rate of GNP per head with measures of increase in life expectancy in European countries*

	1850–1900	1900–29
With absolute increase in life expectancy	−0.02	−0.22
With relative percentage increase	−0.21	−0.36
With percentage decline in longevity shortfall	0.13	0.47

Source: Data of table 5.25 and 5.26. Longevity shortfall was computed from a 'norm' of 65 years

Russia which remained untouched by industrialization also continued to have low levels of life expectancy. If modern economic growth had not occurred, low levels of life expectancy typical of pre-industrial societies would, in all probability, have continued. The weakness of the correlation reflects rather the fact that countries which industrialized early and fast and thereby achieved high rates of economic growth were not necessarily the countries where levels of living, and life expectancy in particular, increased the most. This should affect one's assessment of comparative economic performance. Because of their pre-occupation with the growth rate, economic historians have nearly always compared the French record of economic progress in the nineteenth century unfavourably with the British, and the Netherlands' record unfavourably with that of Belgium. If we take increase in life expectancy as our indicator of progress, these judgements no longer seem appropriate.

This conclusion is also supported by the following consideration. It was pointed out in section 5.1 that the link between increased GNP per head and an improvement in social indicators could be interpreted in several different ways. If we use a narrow, strictly causal version in which GNP per head is regarded merely as a means of achieving increased life expectancy, the ratio of the increment in GNP per head to that in life expectancy at birth in years could be regarded as the cost of an additional year of life expectancy over the relevant period. This interpretation itself is simplistic; rather than increased GNP per head causing life expectancy to increase, both these could be the result of improved living conditions and health; and rather than be regarded as a means of achieving higher life expectancy, increased GNP per head could itself be valued by reason of the greater extent of desire fulfilment that it represents. Nevertheless, inter-country comparison of the 'costs' of achieving an extra year of life expectancy in the sense described could still tell us *something* about variations in the impact of economic growth on levels of living as between European countries during a given period.

It turns out that during the second half of the nineteenth century this 'cost' varied from a minimum of $6.42 for Italy to a maximum of $86.50 for the UK.[18] It is tempting to try to explain this variation in terms of the principle of diminishing returns. The 'cost' should then be higher, the higher the initial level of life expectancy. But this does not appear to be the case. Thus Italy, Germany and the Netherlands all start from very similar levels of (male) life expectancy, the figures being 35.20, 35.59 and 36.40 respectively, but the 'cost' for an extra year of life expectancy for Italy is less than a fifth of that for Germany and half of the figure for the Netherlands. Similarly, Norway and Sweden both start the period with higher life expectancy than the UK, but the 'cost' figure for the UK is between three and four times as much as that for either of these two countries.

The results thus suggest, in particular, a drastic re-appraisal of British industrialization. Britain was the first country to achieve modern economic growth based on an Industrial Revolution. The British experience has exerted enormous influence both on economic development elsewhere and on the development of economics itself. Both by enthusiasts and critics, it has been regarded as *the* model of capitalist development. By the former, Britain's industrial growth has been fervently admired as the unbinding of Prometheus, as a flowering of 'the European miracle' and so on. Critics, on the other hand, have found in Britain a demonstration of the inequities of capitalism. Marx based his analysis of capitalism on his reading of the British experience. Many of his followers have looked on this experience as showing that capitalism was incapable of improving levels of living for the masses of the people. And in general, complaints against capitalist economic growth, or even against economic growth as such, remain to this day highly coloured by the British experience.[19] But, in terms of raising levels of living, pre-twentieth-century British economic performance was a rather poor one by European standards. Identifying British capitalism with capitalism itself could be misleading, for there were considerable differences *among* European countries in this respect. Just *why* this was so is not clear. 'More markets', it appears, did not ensure rapid growth in levels of living (as the British case testifies). Social infrastructure was perhaps more important. There was a marked contrast in this regard between say, Britian and Belgium on the one hand and the Scandinavian countries on the other, decidedly to the latter's advantage, especially in housing and elementary education.[20] And late industrializing countries seem to have done better in terms of raising life expectancy than those where the Industrial Revolution first started.

Apart from comparing European countries among themselves we may also be interested in comparing past experience of European countries as a group with that of developing countries in a more recent period. A few points of similarity between current economic development in developing countries and that of European countries in the past have already been noted. Some other points of comparison will be considered now. One is the initial level of per capita income. There is a considerable literature on the relative backwardness of the developing countries today as compared to the developed countries in their pre-industrial phase. The dominant view has been that the former come off much worse in the comparison. Contemporary developing countries are, it is said, starting from a much lower level of income per head than did European countries in a corresponding phase in the past. Precise discussion of this view is rendered difficult by the differences that exist among its exponents on 'sampling' (the list of countries included in the comparison), periodization (which 'pre-industrial' or 'correspond-ing' phase is regarded as relevant) and estimation (especially of past GNP per head). Extravagant claims made in the literature, notably Kuznets' that 'the pre-industrial level in the developed countries was several times that of most underdeveloped countries today' will hardly bear much scrutiny.[21] A more reliable picture emerges from the careful calculations of Bairoch which have led him to conclude that 'Europe's GNP per capita before industrialization began was some 30 percent higher than that of Asia and Africa around 1950'.[22] However, GNP per head also varied a great deal within each of these two groups of countries, and in consequence, *some* developing countries had a GNP per head much higher than *some* countries of the other group. Past and present developing countries are not, therefore, far apart, contrary to what has been usually supposed. This makes a comparison of their growth rates more interesting than it would have been otherwise, and to this I now turn.

It is a commonplace in popular writing in the West that 'developing countries' is a mere euphemism. Most of these countries, it is said, have experienced economic stagnation, or even economic decline, since they became free from colonial rule. In more scholarly writing, especially by Marxists, recent economic growth in the Third World is often seen as but a pale shadow of the Industrial Revolution.[23] Arguing against the latter view Little has recently pointed out that in East Asia capitalism has produced ' . . . results that make its nineteenth-century performance look like that of a donkey';[24] but East Asia could still be regarded as 'the exception that proves the rule'. A more comprehensive account of the magnitude of recent economic growth in developing countries, as compared to past European experience, is provided by table 5.29.

This account is not entirely reassuring. Indeed, it has a very disturbing aspect: in several developing countries GNP per head was lower in 1982 than it had been in 1960. Although such countries are unrepresentative of the general trend and accounted for only about 3 per cent of the total population in 1982, the absolute number of people living there is by no means negligible. Further, no country in Europe had experienced negative economic growth over either of the two periods described. On the other hand, table 5.29 gives no support to the prophets of gloom. Growth rates of 2 per cent or more per year were experienced by nearly 62 per cent of the total population of our developing countries. The corresponding percentage in European countries (out of a much smaller aggregate population) was negligible in both the periods considered.

Comparisons based on table 5.29 suffer from the limitation

TABLE 5.29 *Growth rates of GNP per head experienced by people of European countries, 1850–1900 and 1900–1929 and of developing countries, 1960–1982*

Growth rates (% per year)	European countries, per cent of population affected		Developing countries, per cent of population affected, 1960–82
	1850–1900	1900–29	
<0	0.00	0.00	3.42
0 and <1	60.07	72.88	4.08
1 and <1.5	38.00	3.48	29.86
1.5 and <2	1.93	21.58	0.74
2 and over	0.00	2.06	61.90
	100.00	100.00	100.00

Sources: Computed from data given in Bairoch, 'Europe's gross national product, 1800–1975', tables 4, 6, 10 and 12, and in our tables 5.1 and 5.17

that the time periods considered are of unequal duration. In comparing growth rates of GNP per head, the length of the time period over which they are computed could however be important. The shorter the period, the greater inter-country differences is yearly growth rates are expected to be, while over long periods, these differences often turn out to be fairly small. Also, for a particular country the yearly growth rate estimated over a long period, of say 50–60 years, tends to be lower than that for a 10–20 year period. For these reasons, while observing that growth rates of per capita output in developing countries since 1960 are higher than those for the 'take-off' period of the developed countries, Bairoch has argued that the comparison may not be valid 'since it is one between medium-term rates of growth in developing countries and very long-term rates in the developed ones'.[25] But this objection is easily taken care of. Growth rates for developing countries that have been used in this chapter are for the period 1960–82. Table 5.30 presents growth rates of most European countries for four different 20-year periods during 1850–1900; their growth rates for two earlier 20-year periods are reported in table 5.31; and the percentage distribution of the population according to growth rates

TABLE 5.30   *Growth rates of GNP per head in European countries during 20-year periods, 1850–1900 (per cent per year)*

	1850–70	1870–90	1860–80	1880–1900
Austria–Hungary	0.38	0.85	0.45	1.38
Belgium	1.65	0.49	0.92	1.02
Bulgaria	—	—	0.00	0.20
Denmark	1.43	1.97	1.50	2.37
Finland	1.62	0.81	1.54	1.32
France	1.37	0.82	1.21	1.33
Germany	1.63	1.16	1.12	1.85
Italy	0.60	0.00	0.16	0.37
Netherlands	0.85	0.74	0.91	0.63
Norway	0.93	1.09	0.73	1.10
Russia	1.80	−1.58	1.16	0.51
Spain	0.25	−0.12	−0.34	0.42
Sweden	0.77	1.87	1.50	2.04
Switzerland	1.71	1.26	1.73	0.75
United Kingdom	1.59	1.12	0.99	1.30

Source: Computed from data given in Bairoch, 'Europe's gross national product, 1800–1975', table 6, p. 286

experienced during 1840–60, and during 1850–70, is reported in table 5.32.

These figures show that growth rates varied sharply from one 20-year period to another, even as between the two overlapping periods 1840–60 and 1850–70. Over a longer period, 1850–1900 in particular, such fluctuations were smoothed out to a considerable extent. Hence, the choice of the period would certainly affect our comparison. However, for most of the countries concerned, as well as for their combined population, it is the period 1850–70 that shows the highest growth rates, and even as compared to these, growth rates in developing countries during the period 1960–82 look fairly impressive. It is fair to conclude that growth rates of GNP per head experienced recently by people of developing countries have, on the whole, been at least as high as those affecting Europeans during their industrial take-off, and possibly much higher.

If we look at improvements in life expectancy, rather than the

TABLE 5.31   *Growth rates of GNP per head in European countries during 1830–1850 and 1840–1860 (per cent per year)*

	1830–50	1840–60
Austria–Hungary	0.62	0.40
Belgium	1.67	1.77
Denmark	1.04	1.35
Finland	0.95	0.81
France	1.17	0.95
Germany	1.15	1.42
Italy	0.22	0.54
Netherlands	1.04	0.84
Norway	1.12	1.38
Russia	0.15	0.23
Spain	0.87	0.92
Sweden	0.42	0.64
Switzerland	1.76	2.12
United kingdom	1.41	1.76

Source: Bairoch, 'Europe's gross national product, 1800–1975', table 6

growth rate, the superiority of the developing countries' performance is much more marked. Between 1850 and 1900, out of eight European countries for which reliable figures are available, only one shows an increase in male life expectancy at birth of 10 years or more and even for the period 1900–29, only eight out of 15 showed an increase of this magnitude. Against this, in as many as 19 out of the 26 developing countries listed in table 5.1, life expectancy at birth rose by 10 years or more between 1960 and 1982. Comparisons of this kind must, of course, be treated with a great deal of caution. For one thing, the European 'developing countries' of the nineteenth century did not all start their industrial revolution at the same point of time; the 'take-off' point varied. So did their rates of growth. And the same is true of the developing countries of today. Hence, comparing growth performance of the former group of countries during a given period (such as 1850–1900) and that of the latter during another (1960–82), oversimplifies history. Perhaps a more

TABLE 5.32 *Growth rates of GNP per head experienced by European people in some 20-year periods*

Growth rates (% per year)	Per cent of population affected 1840–60	1850–70
<0	0.00	0.00
0 and <1	72.79	29.69
1 and <1.5	14.21	13.36
1.5 and <2	12.10	56.95
2 and over	0.90	0.00
	100.00	100.00

Source: derived from Bairoch, 'Europe's gross national product, 1800–1975', tables 4, 6

important point is that, whether we are comparing rates of growth or improvements in life expectancy, the comparison is really not just between groups of countries but also *between* time periods. Technical possibilities that are available to humankind at the present time far exceed those available in the last century. Hence, the relatively favourable showing by *recent* developing countries is just what one would expect. What this suggests is *not* that all is well with the developing countries (for they could well have done much better), but rather that economic progress does occur. This leads me to the first of three brief remarks of a more general nature with which I shall conclude this book.

5.4 Concluding Remarks

My first remark is about the concept of progress. Bertrand Russell once observed that, often, a disagreement among scholars that appears to turn on some highly technical point, really arises from a difference in conception or outlook that is not stated as an explicit part of the argument at all. Certainly this is so in economics. In much of economic argument, the occurrence of progress is taken for granted. The concept of progress is basic to the present study also and I have appealed to it at several points.

By progress, I do not mean that every day and in every way things are getting better and better. What I have in mind is that individuals and groups of individuals are capable of learning by experience (their own and others'), and normally they will try to exercise this capability. The transmission of knowledge across generations and space, hence progress, is possible because of this. The analysis in this book of such topics as the nature of individual preference orderings, the contribution of imported technology and the moral relevance of literacy or life expectancy as indicators of the level of living is derived in some way from *this* understanding. Hence, our analysis will, and ought to, be rejected by those who reject the concept of progress itself. I, for one, can only agree with Medawar that, 'To deride the hope of progress is the ultimate fatuity, the last word in poverty of spirit and meanness of mind',[26] characteristics which are evident in much of the literature asserting the impossibility of economic development.

My second point is about economic policy. Neither economic theory nor the facts of history can provide the developing countries with any magic formula for bringing about growth, development or welfare. And the question, what is the 'optimal' degree of State intervention in the economy, does not admit of any *general* solution, though particular solutions will often exist. There is now clear evidence that in many developing countries lesser direct intervention in the economy by the State and greater use of decentralized decision making would contribute towards a higher level of living.[27] But this is only part of the story, for achieving higher levels of living may also require *more*, and more effective, State participation and investment in social infrastructure: in health, housing, education and law and order; and in many cases, it will require, above all else, steps to ensure that the policies of the State do not merely serve the interests of a tiny and privileged minority.

My last remark concerns the 'holistic' view. Implicit in much of the argument of this book is the judgement that human behaviour is specific and differentiated and can be broken up into separate compartments, economic theory providing one such compartment, which a judicious choice of assumptions could help make more spacious. Others believe that human behaviour can only be viewed as a whole. Every aspect of human behaviour being tied to every other, the analysis of any one aspect, such as the economic, is, on this view, impossible. Some 'holistic' arguments favoured by sociologists and historians were considered, and rejected, earlier in this book. But, in a different way, much of mainstream economics bears the imprint of holism, as well. It is this that explains the persistence of the notion that, given sufficient ingenuity and computer time, *all* aspects of wellbeing could be aggregated into *one* over-all index and different social states compared in terms of it. I believe that such a view is mistaken.

Notes

Introduction

1   John Roberts, *Revolution and Improvement*, London, Weidenfeld and Nicholson, 1976, p. 225.
2   For example, William Nordhaus and James Tobin, 'Is growth obsolete'? in National bureau of Economic Research, *Fiftieth Anniversary Colloquium*, New York, Columbia University Press, 1972.
3   An early attempt at international comparison of levels of living in terms of physical indices is M. K. Bennett, 'International disparities in consumption levels', *American Economic Review*, September 1951. The use of non-monetary indices for this purpose is criticized in W. Beckerman, *International Comparisons of Real Incomes*, OECD, Paris, 1966 (see specially pp. 9–10) and in W. Beckerman and R. Bacon, 'International comparisons of income levels: A suggested new measure', *Economic Journal*, September 1966. A recent account is OECD, *Measuring Social Well-being: A progress report on the development of social indicators*, Paris, 1976.

Chapter 1 Economic Growth and Welfare

1   See for example, H. Cantril, *The Pattern of Human Concerns*, New Brunswick, Rutgers University Press, 1965; Richard A. Easterlin, 'Does economic growth improve the human lot? Some empirical evidence' in Paul H. David and Melvin W. Reder (eds) *Nations and Households in Economic Growth, Essays in Honor of Moses Abramovitz*, New York, Academic Press, 1974; David Morawetz et al. 'Income distribution and self-rated happiness: Some empirical evidence', *Economic Journal*, September 1977; R. Layard, 'Human satisfactions and public policy', *Economic Journal*, December 1980.
2   Cantril, *The Pattern of Human Concerns*, p. 202.

176

3   Easterlin, *Nations and Households in Economic Growth*, p. 115, 'It is a well-accepted dictum among social scientists other than economists that attitudes or "tastes" are a product of the socialization experience of the individual'.
4   Easterlin, *Nations and Households in Economic Growth*, p. 116.
5   The same observation applies to statements about their aspirations by poor people in Soviet Russia during the 1930s, reported in A. R. Luria's classic study of *Cognitive Development: Its Cultural and Social Foundations*, edited by Michael Cole, Cambridge, Massachusetts and London, Harvard University Press, 1976. For instance, an illiterate 38-year-old man from a mountain pasture camp situated in a remote area of Russia was asked 'Are you satisfied with yourself or would you like to be different?', and answers 'It would be good if I had a little more land and could sow some wheat' (p. 150).
6   Cantril, *The Pattern of Human Concerns*, p. 292.
7   J. F. C. Harrison, *The Common People*, London, Fontana Paperbacks, 1984, p. 385. It is usually found in enquiries of this kind that people tend to emphasize the 'objective' characteristics of consumer durables such as a reduction of drudgery and increased flexibility (especially for female members of the household) and often state explicitly that they would have been much better off in the past, had they had such things then. This is quite different from the scenario proposed by Jon Elster in the course of his analysis of induced changes in preference orderings. 'We were happier before we got these fancy new things, although now we would be miserable without them.' ('Sour grapes – utilitarianism and the genesis of wants', in Amartya Sen and Bernard Williams (eds), *Utilitarianism and Beyond*, Cambridge, Cambridge University Press, 1980, p. 233). Harrison's perceptive remarks provide a much-needed corrective to the pessimistic view of economic growth now in fashion. 'It is easy', he points out 'to take a superior and rather hypocritical view about the spread of materialism and to lament the loss of those virtues of stoicism and self-denial which nourished the old labour movement. But we shall probably be on firmer ground if we emphasize the positive gains which affluence brought through an increase in both comfort and freedom' (ibid., p. 385). Again, 'consumerism' has almost become a dirty word. Yet, as Harrison observes, 'Consumerism provided one of the few areas in which a majority of ordinary people had the power to make real choices and decisions affecting their daily lives. To that extent it was valued as an enlargement of freedom' (p. 386). In similar vein, Robert J. Smith (*Japanese Society: Tradition, self and the social order*, Cambridge, Cambridge University Press, 1983) points out that people want better schools and hospitals and refrigeration to relieve domestic drudgery, and package-tour holidays, 'not because their minds have been brainwashed and their tastes contrived by advertising but because the things are desirable' (p. 104).
8   For a succint account, see Arthur J. Taylor, *Laissez-faire and State*

Intervention in Nineteenth-century Britain, London and Basingstoke, Macmillan, 1972, which also has an excellent bibliography.

9   Jacob Viner, '*Adam Smith and Laissez-faire*' reprinted in J. M. Clark (ed.) *Adam Smith 1766–1926*, Chicago, University of Chicago Press, 1928. On this point, J. M. Keynes' *The End of Laissez-faire*, London, Hogarth Press, 1926, is also instructive. Keynes notes, for example, that the phrase *laissez-faire* is not to be found in the works of Adam Smith, of Ricardo or of Malthus. 'Even the idea', he goes on, 'is not present in a dogmatic form in any of these authors' (p. 20). This last statement however, appears to slur over an important distinction in this regard as between Smith on the one hand and Ricardo and Malthus on the other.

10   Adam Smith, *The Wealth of Nations*, edited by R. H. Campbell and A. S. Skinner, vol. 2, p. 687, Oxford, Clarendon Press, 1976. All subsequent references to this book are also to the same edition.

11   T. C. Koopmans, *Three Essays on the State of Economic Science*, New York, Toronto and London, McGraw Hill Book Company, 1957, p. 49. Confusion regarding what precisely is being claimed is still quite prevalent, however. 'A bad nomenclature (Pareto optimum) in the literature, together with much carelessness in textbooks, often misleads people into thinking that there is some theorem which claims that a competitive equilibrium is socially optimal. There is no such claim' (Frank Hahn, 'General equilibrium theory', in *The Crisis in Economic Theory*, edited by Daniel Bell and Irving Kristol, New York, Basic Books, 1982, p. 126).

12   As Arrow has shown, the number of markets required for perfect competition, in the relevant sense, to exist would be less if contingencies could be traded, e.g. through a security market, but this does not really make the definition of perfect competition less demanding. How very demanding making such a judgement would be, has not usually been recognized in the literature of general equilibrium theory. An exceptionally clear account of the issues involved is provided in E. Malinvaud's elegant textbook, *Lectures on Micro-economic Theory*, Amsterdam, North-Holland, 1972. Perfect competition is said to prevail 'if the price of each good is the same for all agents and all transactions, if each agent considers this price as independent of his own decisions, and if he feels able to acquire or dispose of any quantity of goods at this price' (p. 106). This definition, the author adds in a footnote, 'is sufficient for the theoretical model to be discussed but not for a typology of real situations, since it does not define the required conditions for a competitive equilibrium to be realised' (p. 106).

13   See Ajit K. Dasgupta and D. W. Pearce, *Cost–Benefit Analysis: Theory and practice*, London, Macmillan, 1972, chapter 5.

14   Relevant issues are discussed in Werner Hildebrand (ed.) *Advances in Economic Theory*, Cambridge, Cambridge University Press, 1982, Part I: Economics of incentives.

15   See also n. 26.

16   An up-to-date and highly readable account of economics for beginners by

Rupert Pennant-Rea and Clive Crook, *The Economist Economics*, Harmondsworth, Penguin Books, 1986 (an account which is certainly not biased against free enterprise) concludes chapter 14, on Welfare and Efficiency, with the observation that ' . . . even if the theoretical support for free markets is less strong than it seems, governments might do much more damage if they are too quick to think they know better' (p. 158). This is not far removed from Adam Smith's pragmatic conclusions described above (p. 8-10); but Smith would probably have added that some governments inflict much more damage than others.

17 Some useful second-best rules have, however, been prescribed in the literature on the trade policy. See, for example, Jagdish Bhagwati, *Trade, Tariffs and Growth*, London, Weidenfeld and Nicholson, 1969.

18 Frank Hahn and Martin Hollis (eds), *Philosophy and Economic Theory*, Oxford, Oxford University Press, 1979, p. 3.

19 Oscar Wilde, *The Importance of Being Earnest*, Act II.

20 Hal Varian, *Micro-economic Theory*, New York, The Macmillan Company, 1982, p. 112.

21 Cf. Amartya Sen, *Choice, Welfare and Measurement*, Oxford, Basil Blackwell, 1982, p. 56.

22 Jeremy Bentham, *Of Laws in General*, edited by H. L. A. Hart, London, Athlone Press, 1970, p. 70, footnote. The same point had been made by Bishop Butler in an article that appeared in 1726 criticizing Mandeville's theory that all action is motivated by self-love: 'And if because every particular affection is a man's own, and the pleasure arising from its gratification his own pleasure . . . such particular affection must be called self-love; according to this way of speaking, no creature can possibly act but merely from self-love; and every action and every affection whatever is to be resolved up into this one principle. But then this is not the language of mankind' (quoted in *The Fable of the Bees* by Bernard Mandeville, with a Commentary by F. B. Kay, second volume, Oxford, Clarendon Press, 1924, p. 129).

23 Adam Smith, *Theory of Moral Sentiments*, edited by D. D. Raphael and A. L. Macfie, Oxford, Clarendon Press, 1976, p. 309. A similar view of human motivation is presented by 'Lui' in Diderot's classic dialogue, *Le Neveu de Rameau*.

24 *Theory of Moral Sentiments*, p. 302.

25 J. E. Cairnes, *Some Leading Principles of Political Economy*, London, Macmillan, 1874, p. 725.

26 David Hume, 'Of the dignity or meanness of human nature', *The Philosophical Works of David Hume*, Boston, Little Brown and Company and Edinburgh, Adam and Charles Black, vol. III, p. 91.

27 In an authoritative study, J. Green and J. J. Laffont report that ' . . . there is no empirical study in which a strong tendency towards free rider behaviour is in evidence' (*Incentives in Public Decision Making*, Amsterdam, North Holland, 1979, p. 185). This judgement is confirmed by subsequent

research, for example by Gerald Maxwell and Ruth E. Ames, 'Economists free ride, does anyone else?' *Journal of Public Economics*, vol. 15, 1981,pp. 295–310 and Peter Bohm, 'Revealing demand for an actual public good', *Journal of Public Economics*, vol. 24, 1981, p. 135–51.

28 *The Republic*, Book II, 359, translated by Benjamin Jowett.

29 Jacques Monod, *Chance and Necessity*, Collins, Fontana Books, 1974, p. 156.

30 See on this point Howard Margolis, *Selfishness, Altruism and Rationality, A Theory of Social Choice*, Cambridge, Cambridge University Press, 1982, p. 31.

31 P. B. Medawar, *The Future of Man*, London, Methuen, 1960, p. 99.

32 Knut Wicksell, *Lectures on Political Economy*, edited by Lional Robbins, London, Allen and Unwin, vol. 1, 1934, pp. 9–10.

33 *The Wealth of Nations*, vol. 1, pp. 26–7. The point has been missed by most critics. An exception is Gertrude Himmelfarb, who observes that self-interest for Smith was not a moral principle as lofty as altruism ' . . . but in the mundane affairs of life (the provision of dinner) more reliable and effective' (*The Idea of Poverty: England in the early industrial age*, London, Faber, 1984, p. 40).

34 F. Y. Edgeworth, *Mathematical Psychics: An essay on the application of mathematics to the moral sciences*, London, Kegan Paul, 1881, p. 16.

35 Thus, according to Stephan Körner (*Experience and Conduct*, Cambridge, Cambridge University Press, 1976, p. 175), although ordinarily, in the analysis of practical economic conduct, it may be harmless, even useful, to take only first-level preferences, i.e. those undominated by higher level prudential or moral ones, into account, ' . . . it is simply a gross error to regard the maximisation of first level preferences as the supreme principle of rational conduct. It is, therefore, encouraging to notice that, unlike their classical predecessors, at least some contemporary economists tend to restrict the applicability of the principle to more narrowly economic contexts'. Two comments are in order. First, a well-defined stratification of preferences need not exist. Secondly, no classical economist of repute, least of all Adam Smith, regarded first-level preferences based on self-interest as the supreme principle of rational conduct.

36 Yet another interpretation of the assumption self-interest has been offered by Kenneth J. Arrow and F. H. Hahn, *General Competitive Analysis*, 1972, pp. VI–VII: 'There is by now a long and fairly imposing line of economists from Adam Smith to the present who have sought to show that a decentralized economy motivated by self-interest and guided by price signals would be compatible with a coherent disposition of economic resources that could be regarded, in a well-defined sense, as superior to a large class of possible alternative dispositions. Moreover, the price signals would operate in a way to establish this degree of coherence . . . The proposition having been put forward and very seriously entertained, it is important to know not only whether it is true, but also whether it *could* be

true.' On this interpretation the assumption has nothing to do with actual economic behaviour but merely describes properties of a possible world. This is certainly not the way Adam Smith, and indeed most economists, have looked at the matter. For the difficulties involved in this interpretation, and a clear general account of the role of assumptions in economic theory, see Alan Musgrave, 'Unreal assumptions in economic theory: the F-twist untwisted', *Kyklos*, vol. 34, 1981, Fase 3.

37 Graaff regards 'a person's choices or general welfare, as determined by a large number of variables, some of which have traditionally interested economists and some of which have not'. He calls the former 'economic variables'. 'Welfare economics then proceeds on the assumption that the non-economic ones all remain unchanged. They can be thought of as exogenous variables – that is, as influencing economic variables without being influenced by them.' J. De Graaff, *Theoretical Welfare Economics*, Cambridge, Cambridge University Press, 1957, pp. 5–6.

38 Nassau Senior, *Industrial Efficiency and Social Economy*, London, P. S. King & Son, vol. 1, 1928, pp. 72–7.

39 Ibid., p. 76. On this point, the views of Senior and of classical political economists in general were no different from those of Marx and Engels: cf. 'In a word, the workers' dwellings of Manchester are dirty, miserable and wholly lacking in comforts. In such houses only inhuman, degraded and unhealthy creatures would feel at home'. Engels, *The Condition of the Working Class in England*, translated and edited by W. O. Henderson and W. H. Chaloner, Oxford, Basil Blackwell, 1971, p. 75.

40 Cf. Alfred Marshall, *Principles of Economics*, 9th (Variorium) edn, (first edition published 1890), London Macmillan, 1961, p. 2.

41 Ibid., p. 2.

42 Ibid., p. 2.

43 Ibid., p. 3.

44 Ibid., p. 4. Marshall surely reflects not merely his own predilection or the temper of this time, but also the temper of economics itself in pointing out that although the dignity of man had been proclaimed by the Christian religion, it is only 'now' that we are starting seriously to enquire whether 'the lower classes' are really necessary, i.e. 'whether there need be a large number of people doomed from their birth to hard work in order to provide for others the requisites of a refined and cultured life; while they themself are prevented by their poverty and toil from having any share in that life' (ibid., p. 3).

45 See Ajit K. Dasgupta and D. W. Pearce, *Cost Benefit Analysis: Theory and practice*, London, Macmillan, 1972, chapter 5; and Ajit K. Dasgupta and M. N. Murty, 'Economic evaluation of water pollution abatement: A case study of the paper and pulp industry in India', *Indian Economic Review*, vol. XX, no. 2.

46 Robert Paul Wolff, 'The derivation of the minimum state' in Jeffrey Paul (ed.), *Reading Nozick*, Oxford, Basil Blackwell, 1982, pp. 98–9.

47 A useful account of different kinds of comparability of welfare among persons is to be found in two papers by Amartya Sen, 'Interpersonal aggregation and partial comparability' and 'Interpersonal comparisons of welfare', both included in his *Choice, Welfare and Measurement*, Oxford, Blackwell, 1982. We are concerned here with a different issue, namely the comparability of welfare derived from different groups of alternatives by the same person, but there are many common problems as between the two contexts.

Chapter 2 The Determination of Individual Preferences

1 Notably, Amartya Sen, 'Rational fools: A critique of the behavioural foundations of economic theory', reprinted in *Choice, Welfare and Measurement*, Oxford, Blackwell, 1982.

2 Philip Pettit (ed.), 'Rational man theory', in Christopher Hookway and Philip Pettit, *Action and Interpretation*, Cambridge, Cambridge University Press, 1978, p. 58.

3 B. F. Skinner, *Science and Human Behavior*, New York, The Macmillan Company, 1953, p. 419.

4 Paul J. Poppen and Abraham Wandersman with Lois P. Wandersman, 'What are humanism and behaviorism and what can they say to one another?' in Abraham Wandersman, Paul J. Poppenham and David T. Ricks (eds), *Humanism and Behaviorism: Dialogue and growth*, Oxford, Pergamon Press, 1976.

5 A standard recent discussion of the issues involved is by P. K. O'Brien and S. L. Engerman, 'Changes in income and its distribution during the Industrial Revolution', in Roderick Floud and Donald McCloskey (eds), *The Economic History of Britain since 1700*, vol. 1, Cambridge, Cambridge University Press, 1981. The authors ask the question: 'To what extent can movement to urban areas be regarded as voluntary in response to the higher urban than rural wages?' (p. 116). The answer, roughly, is that it can, though their statement (p. 130) that 'voluntary migration to cities and decisions to increase labour input may have reflected individual preferences at the time', appears to be tautological since a 'voluntary' decision *means* one reflecting individual preferences. They add that a correct answer could depend on the actual mix of voluntary acceptance and compulsion that was involved in the creation of an industrial work discipline. That the limits of 'compulsion' cannot be precisely defined does not imply that the distinction itself is meaningless.

6 John Stuart Mill, *On Liberty*, Harmondsworth, Penguin Books, 1974 (first published 1859), p. 122.

7 B. F. Skinner, *Reflections on Behaviorism and Society*, Englewood Cliffs, New Jersey, Prentice-Hall, 1978, p. 5.

8   B. E. Skinner, *Cumulative Record*, enlarged edition, New York, Appleton-Century-Crofts, 1961, p. 27.

9   Skinner, *Reflections*, p. 51.

10 Skinner, *Reflections*, p. 51.

11 Skinner, *Reflections*, p. 55.

12 An elegant discussion of the possibilities and limitations of this approach is to be found in Kaushik Basu, *Revealed Preference of Governments*, Cambridge, Cambridge University Press, 1979.

13 Cf. Pettit, *Action and Interpretation*.

14 A. K. Sen, *Collective Choice and Social Welfare*, San Francisco, Holden-Day, and Edinburgh and London, Oliver and Boyd, 1970, p. 34.

15 Steven Lukes, *Individualism*, Oxford, Basil Blackwell, 1973, p. 118.

16 Cf. 'The concept of a free, responsible individual is embedded in our language and pervades our practices, codes and beliefs . . .. A scientific formulation, on the other hand is new and strange', Skinner, *Science and Human and Behaviour*, p. 10.

17 Philip Pettit (*Judging Justice*, London, Routledge and Kegan Paul, 1980, p. 49) argues that 'It is because he thinks of institutions as involving nothing more than people that the individualist unquestioningly takes them to be answerable to the interests of individuals'. This may indeed be a true description of the behaviour of 'unquestioning' individualists but the ethical judgement that social institutions and arrangements should be assessed by the criterion of how far they promote the wellbeing of individuals does not necessarily imply a denial of the ontological status of institutions.

18 The determinist might of course concede the possibility of such interaction but still refuse to give it much importance on the ground that inter-action itself can occur only to the extent that the culture permits. However, this kind of objection appears to be based on circular reasoning. If some cultures permit more interaction than others, and certain kinds of development tend to help change a culture from being one of the latter to one of the former sort, the possibilities of interaction are increased!

19 M. I. Finley (*The Use and Abuse of History*, London, Chatto and Windus, 1975, p. 127) observes that the ancient Greek belonged not just to 'Hellas', but to a multiplicity of groups, the interests of which were often conflicting, and that an individual's ties, whether institutional or psychological, to each such group varied substantially according to the context or activity, his status within the group, his own aspirations and so on. This is true of *all* societies.

20 Eric Hobsbawm, 'Introduction: Inventing traditions', in Eric Hobsbawm and Terence Ranger (eds), *The Invention of Traditions*, Cambridge, Cambridge University Press, 1983, p. 1.

21 F. M. Fisher and K. Shell, *The Economic Theory of Prices Indices*, New York and London, Academic Press, 1972; Amartya Sen, 'The welfare basis of

real income comparisons: A survey', *Journal of Economic Literature*, March, 1979.

22 R. M. Hartwell, *The Industrial Revolution and Economic Growth*, London, Methuen, 1971, p. 11. For a critique of such views, see Ajit K. Dasgupta, *Economic Theory and the Developing Countries*, London, Macmillan, 1974, chapter 1.

23 Hartwell, *The Industrial Revolution and Economic Growth*, p. 11.

24 J. H. Boeke, *The Structure of the Netherlands Indian Economy*, New York, Institute of Pacific Relations, 1942.

25 Ibid., p. 92.

26 Ibid., p. 94.

27 R. H. Tawney, *Land and Labour in China*, London, Allen and Unwin, 1932, p. 19.

28 Grahame Clark and Stuart Piggot, *Prehistoric Society*, London, Hutchinson, 1965, p. 223.

29 Ibid., p. 224. A somewhat different interpretation is given by those who reject the hypothesis of the diffusion of technology and favour instead that of independent re-discovery. For a critique of the anti-diffusionist thesis, currently in fashion among archaeologists, see Bruce G. Trigger, *Time and Traditions: Essays in archaeological interpretation*, Edinburgh, Edinburgh University Press, 1978, pp. 216–28.

30 Grahame Clark, *World Prehistory, A New Outline*, Cambridge, Cambridge University Press, 1969, p. 126; Stuart Piggot's paper on Early Towns in Europe in P. R. S. Moorey (ed.), *The Origins of Civilisation*, Oxford, Clarendon Press, 1979 is also of some relevance here. Piggot points out that unlike in West Asia, in early Europe up to as late as the third millennium BC there are no signs of development: 'Although continuity of settlement is maintained by a competent system of agriculture, excepting in metallurgy, no development can be traced in the sequence of material culture which would lead us to infer any changes within the social order, whereby as in Mesopotamia for instance we can with justice talk of the evolution from village to town to city' (pp. 43–4).

31 Charles Singer (ed.), *A History of Technology*, Oxford, Clarendon Press, vol. 2, 1954, p. 756. This contrasts with Boeke's views quoted above.

32 Thanks largely to Joseph Needham, *Science and Civilization in China*, Cambridge, Cambridge University Press, 1954. An excellent discussion is also to be found in Mark Elvin, *The Pattern of the Chinese Past*, Stanford, Stanford University Press, 1973.

33 Ernest Gellner, *Relativism and the Social Sciences*, Cambridge, Cambridge University Press, 1985, p. 98.

34 See V. A. Mahler, *Dependence Approaches to International Political Economy*, New York, Columbia University Press, 1980 and Ian M. D. Little, *Economic Development: Theory, policy and international relatins*, New York, Basic Books, 1982.

35 Grahame Clark, *The Identity of Man*, London and New York, Methuen, 1985, p. 159.

Chapter 3 The Justification of Social Indicators

1 The clearest discussion of the issues involved is in J. de V. Graaff, *Theoretical Welfare Economics*, Cambridge, Cambridge University Press, 1957.

2 See for example, Phyllis Deane, *The First Industrial Revolution*, Cambridge, Cambridge University Press, 1967, pp. 249–50; Peter Matthias, *The First Industrial Nation*, London, Methuen, 1969, p. 218.

3 According to this theory, states Derek Parfit, 'certain things are good or bad for people, whether or not these people would want to have the good things, or to avoid the bad things'. (*Reasons and Persons*, Oxford, Clarendon Press, p. 499). Others would deny that such a list is at all possible, among them Philippa Foot, who claims that 'there is no such thing as an objectively good state of affairs'. *Proceedings of the Aristotelian Society*, Supplement, 1972, reprinted in J. Raz (ed.), *Practical Reasoning*, Oxford, Oxford University Press, 1978, p. 183.

4 Paul Streeten, *First Things First, Meeting Basic Human Needs in Developing Countries*, New York, Oxford University Press, 1981, p. 25.

5 Robert Nozick, *Anarchy, State and Utopia*, Oxford, Basil Blackwell, 1974, pp. 234–5.

6 For example, Brian Barry, *Political Argument*, London, Routledge and Kegan Paul, 1965, p. 48; A. J. Culyer, *Need and the National Health Service: Economics and social choice*, London, Martin Robertson, 1976, p. 14; Alan White, *Modal Thinking*, Oxford, Basil Blackwell, 1975.

7 White, *Modal Thinking*.

8 J. Milton, 'Of education' *The Portable Milton*, Harmondsworth, Penguin Books, 1977, pp. 136 and 137.

9 A. J. Culyer, *Need and the National Health Service*.

10 Streeten, *First Things First*, p. 25.

11 An interesting discussion of the significance of this fact for pre-Socratic theories of pleasure can be found in J. C. B. Gosling and C. C. W. Taylor, *The Greeks on Pleasure*, Oxford, Clarendon Press, 1982, pp. 24–5.

12 B. F. Skinner, *Science and Human Behavior*, New York, The Macmillan Press, 1953, p. 235.

13 See, for example, Indira Rajaraman, 'Poverty, inequality and economic growth: Rural Punjab, 1960–61 to 1970–71', *Journal of Development Studies*, July 1975.

14 For this reason 'good' indices of inequality are required to be mean (or scale) independent. See Nanak C. Kakwani, *Income Inequality and Poverty*, New York, Oxford University Press, 1980, p. 65.

15 Ian M. D. Little, *Economic Development: Theory, policy and interntional relations*, New York, Basic Books, 1982, pp. 215–16.

16 For example C. D. Harbury, 'Inheritance and the distribution of personal wealth in Britain', *Economic Journal*, December 1962; C. D. Harbury and P. C. McMahon, 'Inheritance and the characteristics of top wealth leavers in

Britain', *Economic Journal*, September 1973; Nicholas Oulton, 'Inheritance and the distribution of wealth', *Oxford Economic Papers*, March 1976; J. B. Davies and A. F. Shorrocks, 'Assessing the quantitative importance of inheritance in the distribution of wealth', *Oxford Economic Papers*, March 1978; Ajit K. Dasgupta and S. Paul, 'Inheritance and wealth inequality: The case of the Punjab', Discussion Paper No 86.04, May 1986, Department of Economics, The University of Western Australia.

17 In an earlier period, we are reminded by C. E. G. Clay, *Economic Expansion and Social Change: England 1500–1700*, vol. II, Cambridge, Cambridge University Press, 1984, p. 241, '. . . poor relief was envisaged primarily as a means of maintaining order'. Hegel's suggestion that improvements in administrative efficiency in European countries during the nineteenth century were motivated by ' . . . an amplified fear of popular disorders' (*Lectures on the Philosophy of World History*, Cambridge, Cambridge University Press, 1975, p. 26) seems to me to be highly plausible. Similarly, in a standard text on *The Evolution of the British Welfare State*, London, The Macmillan Press, 2nd edn, 1984, Foreward, p. XXX, Derek Fraser points out that ' . . . the history of social policy is characterised by strong, protest movements and "pressures from without" which often forced the government's hand.. . . Concessions to working class welfare were rarely made through altruism, more often than not it was for fear of something worse'. This was no less true of Germany where the first major step towards state social security legislation of the 1880s, enacted under Bismarck, has been attributed to fears inspired by the Paris Commune (J. Tampke, 'Bismarck's social legislation: A genuine breakthrough?' in W. J. Mommsen (ed.), *The Emergence of the Welfare State in Britain and Germany*, London, Croom Helm, 1981); and its political aims are accurately described by H. P. Ullmann: 'By repression on the one hand and limited concessions in the area of social policy on the other, the aim was to split the Social Democratic workers' movement considered "a danger to the state". The agitators were to be rendered politically impotent and the "good" workers won over for the state by welfare provisions' ('German industry and Bismarck's social security system', in Mommsen, *The Emergence of the Welfare State*, p. 133).

18 It is also implicit in Little's critique of the 'needs' principle, discussed above.

19 Jonathan Bradshaw, 'A taxonomy of social need', in Gordon McLachlan (ed.), *Problems and Progress in Medical Care*, London, New York, Toronto, Oxford University Press, 1972, p. 73.

20 Richard M. Titmuss, *Commitment to Welfare*, London, George Allen and Unwin, 1968, p. 66.

21 Bradshaw, 'A taxonomy of social need', p. 72.

22 Michael Cooper, *Rationing Health Care*, London, Croom Helm, 1975, p. 20.

23 William Shakespeare, *Julius Caesar*, III, (ii), (110).

24   Joanna Mack and Steward Lansley, *Poor Britain*, London, George Allen and Unwin, 1985.

25   Thanks largely to the work of P. V. Sukhatme, especially, 'The world's hunger and future needs in food supplies', *Journal of the Royal Statistical Society*, Series A (General), 1961; and 'The protein problem, its size and nature', *Journal of the Royal Statistical Society*, Series A (General), 1974.

26   See P. V. Sukhatme, 'The incidence of under-nutrition', *Indian Journal of Agricultural Economics*, Conference Number, July–September, 1977; and T. N. Srinivasan, 'Malnutrition: Some measurement and policy issues', *Journal of Development Economics*, vol. 8, 1981, pp. 3–19.

27   Those who assert that there is a stable core of basic needs tend to emphasize the biological component. Thus arguing against the 'alleged variety of needs', Mandel points out that, ' . . . any moderately serious study of anthropology and history will show, on the contrary, how remarkably stable they are; food, clothing, shelter etc. . . . . There are half a dozen needs which do not seem to have changed since the beginnings of homo sapiens'. (E. Mandel, *Marxist Economic Theory*, New York, Monthly Review Press, 1968, p. 660). On the contrary Marx himself regarded even basic needs as socially determined: 'Hunger is hunger, but the hunger gratified by cooked meat eaten with a knife and fork is a different hunger from that which bolts down raw meat with the aid of hand, nail and tooth.' (*Grundrisse*, Harmondsworth, Penguin Books, 1973, p. 92). Broadly interpreted, Marx's statement could be taken to mean that the effective content of basic needs tends to change over a long historical period during which the mode of production is transformed. However, it tends to blur the issues involved by making a universal biological need (to eat) conjoint with the need for a knife and fork to eat with, which is not only culture-specific but also a fairly recent innovation (in England, according to Fernand Braudel, *Capitalism and Material Life 1400–1800*, Fontana/Collins, 1974, p. 139, the use of forks became general only around 1750) and as well, by making it appear as if the difference between eating cooked meat and eating it raw turned on the use of cutlery. Perhaps a more relevant question would be whether the hungers gratified by eating food with knife and fork, with one's fingers or with chopsticks are different hungers. Supposing that they are is a particular instance of a more general failure to distinguish beteen an abstract need and the specific means used in satisfying it. The distinction can be of much practical relevance when one is trying to decide on the basket of goods and services to be used in estimating a poverty line – a point which underlines the following comment by T. N. Madan on a statement by Gunnar Myrdal in *Asian Drama* bewailing the lack of pyjama suits and underwear among South Asians, 'Are these European-style garments a relevant yardstick for tropical Asia? Cannot an Indian sleep in his *Kurta* and *Dhoti* – his working clothes – and yet be clean and comfortable?' (quoted in Morris David Morris, *Measuring the Condition of the World's Poor*, New York, Pergamon Press,

1979, p. 25). The analysis of goods in terms of their 'characteristics' (K. J. Lancaster, 'A new approach to consumer theory', *Journal of Political Economy*, April, 1966) could perhaps be useful here.

28   C. A. R. Crossland, *The Future of Socialism*, London, Jonathan Cape Paperback, 1964, p. 89.

29   Peter Townsend, *Poverty in the United Kingdom*, Harmondsworth, Penguin Books, 1979, p. 31.

30   A precise statement of the assumptions required for a shame-based notion of need to be valid can be found in Gabriele Taylor, *Pride, Shame and Guilt*, Oxford, Clarendon Press, 1985, though her study is not concerned with the concept of need as such. Shame, she points out, requires an audience. 'The agent is seen as deviating from some norm and in feeling shame he will identify with the audience's view and the consequent verdict that he has lost status' (p. 57). Such identification follows logically from the hypothesis that no distinction is possible between 'private' and 'public' aspects of self-respect; a person can assess himself *only* in terms of what others (the relevant honour group) think of him. The framework within which this characterization of shame holds is described by some anthropologists as a 'shame culture'. But 'our' culture may not be such; and even within a 'shame culture', the really poor and needy may not belong to honour groups at all.

31   See Richard C. Trexler, 'Charity and the defense of urban elites in the Italian communes', in Frederick Cople Jaher (ed.), *The Rich, the Well-born and the Powerful, Elites and Upper Classes In History*, Urbana, University of Illinois Press, 1973.

32   John Stuart Mill, *On Liberty*, Harmondsworth, Penguin Books, 1974 (first published 1859), p. 63. Mill warned that 'social tyranny' of this kind could be more formidable than many kinds of political oppression.

33   H. J. McCloskey, 'Rights', *Philosophical Quarterly*, vol. 15, 1965, p. 57.

34   Allen E. Buchanan, 'The right to a decent minimum of health care', *Philosophy and Public Affairs*, Winter 1984, vol. 13, no. 1, p. 57.

35   Charles Fried, *Right and Wrong*, Cambridge, Massachusetts and London, Harvard University Press, 1978, p. 108.

36   Ronald Dworkin, *Taking Rights Seriously*, London, Duckworth, 1978.

37   Robert Nozick, *Anarchy, State and Utopia*, Oxford, Basil Blackwell, 1974, p. 166.

38   Reasons why the concept of equality before the law between individuals belonging to different racial groups long failed to take root in American society are discussed in Don E. Fehrenbacker, *Slavery, Law and Politics, the Dred Scott case in historical perspective*, Oxford, Oxford University Press, 1981, see especially pp. 299–307.

39   C. Fried, *Right and Wrong*, p. 113.

40   See Amartya Sen, *Poverty and Famines*, Oxford, Oxford University Press, 1981.

41 Isaiah Berlin, *Two Concepts of Liberty*, Oxford, Clarendon Press, 1958.
42 Amartya Sen, 'Rights and agency', *Philosophy and Public Affairs*, vol. 11, no. 1.
43 See D. P. Chaudhri and Ajit K. Dasgupta, *Agriculture and the Development Process; The case of Punjab*, London, Croom Helm, 1985.
44 C. Fried, *Right and Wrong*, p. 162.
45 K. G. Willis, *The Economics of Town and Country Planning*, London, Granada, 1980.
46 'A defence of poetry', *Works of Percy Bysshe Shelley*, London, Ernest Benn, New York, Charles Scribner's, vol. VII, p. 122.
47 According to M. I. Finley, *Politics in the Ancient World*, Cambridge, Cambridge University Press, 1983, p. 125, the proposition that slaves, women and barbarians were inferior by nature and hence should be excluded from taking part in discussion, would have been taken as axiomatic by *all* Greeks.
48 Hugh Trevor Roper (*Renaissance Essays*, London, Secker and Warburg, 1985, p. 3) remarks about the followers of Plato: 'Whatever the culture within which they lived and thought – whether ancient or modern, eastern or western, pagan, Christian or Muslim – they invariably produced totalitarian systems repellent to all liberal men.' More to the point, they invariably produced inegalitarian and hierarchical systems.
49 See the introduction by E. R. Dodds to Plato's *Georgias*, Oxford, Clarendon Press, 1959, p. 33.
50 *Georgias*, 507E–519D. The point is that Plato was not simply decrying present evils or remembering vanished glories. His indictment applies to the past as well, to Militiades and Themistocles and Cimon and Pericles.
51 Dodds, *Georgias*, p. 34.
52 Joseph Vogt, *Ancient Slavery and the Ideal of Man*, Oxford, Basil Blackwell, 1974, p. 25.
53 Cf. Vogt, ibid., p. 25, 'Nor should we lose sight of the fact that in industrialized countries, today every productive person is in charge of a machine, which means that he is in charge of two or three dozen technological slaves'. As if this made slavery in some way less reprehensible! Even Finley's writings sometimes show a curiously ambivalent attitude towards slavery. Thus, he writes: 'Slavery is a great evil: there is no reason why a historian should not say that, but to say only that no matter with how much factual backing is a cheap way to score a point on a dead society to the advantage of our own; retrospective indignation is also a way to justify the present' (M. I. Finley, *Ancient Slavery and Modern Ideology*, London, Chatto and Windus, 1980, p. 64). It is not at all clear what 'saying only that' could mean in such a context, especially if it is also given 'much factual backing'; why justifying the present in so far as the present is characterized by an absence of slavery is a bad thing; or how any evaluative statement could be made without scoring points, not necessarily on a 'cardinal' scale (one may describe a situation as

being better than another without being prepared to say how much better it is).

54   The archaeological argument for inequality is stated most clearly by Grahame Clark, 'Primitive man as hunter, fisher, forager and farmer', in P. R. S. Moorey (ed.), *The Origins of Civilisation*, Oxford, Clarendon Press, 1979, especially pp. 19–20. See also his *The Identity of Man*, London and New York, Methuen, 1985, chapter 6.

55   Finley cites two reasons for asserting that there is an 'unbridgable gap' between us and antiquity: 'first, the fact that it was not possible by any means to bring about an equitable society in antiquity, given the poor resources, the low level of technology, the absence of growth possibilities (other than conquest) in the economy, and the absence of the very idea of progress; second, the acceptance of human inequality, and therefore of the necessity of domination, as natural and immutable', 'Utopianism ancient and modern', in *The Use and Abuse of History*, London, Chatto and Windus, 1975, p. 190.

There are degrees of inequity, however, and the fact that a truly equitable society was impossible in antiquity does not imply that a less inequitable one than what did exist was also impossible.

56   Irma Adelman and Cynthia Taft Morris, *Society, Politics and Economic Development: A quantitiative approach*, Baltimore, The Johns Hopkins Press, 1967, p. IX.

57   Social, political and economic indicators in Irma Adelman and Cynthia Taft Morris, *Society, Politics, and Economic Development: A quantitative approach*, Baltimore, John Hopkins Press, 1967: size of the traditional agricultural sector, extent of dualism, extent of urbanization, character of basic social organization, importance of the indigenous middle class, extent of social mobility, extent of literacy, extent of mass communication, degree of cultural and ethnic homogeneity, degree of social tension, crude fertility rate, degree of modernization of outlook, degree of national integration and sense of national unity, extent of centralization of political power, strength of democratic institutions, degree of freedom of political opposition and press, degree of competitiveness of political parties, predominant basis of the political party system, strength of labour movement, political strength of the traditional elite, political strength of the military, degree of administrative efficiency, extent ot leadership commitment to economic development, extent of political stability, per capita GDP in 1961, rate of growth of real per capita GNP: 1950/51–1963/64, abundance of natural resources, gross investment rate, level of modernization of industry, change in degree of industrialization since 1950, character of agricultrual organization and level of modernization of techniques in agriculture.

58   Ian M. D. Little, *Economic Development, Theory, Policy and International Relations*, New York, Basic Books, p. 11.

59   Such a contrast, often drawn by historians and cultural anthropologists,

rests on little more than casual impression, or worse. (See also chapter 2.) Thus Chinese culture has been described as 'holistic' and 'organic', one in which the individual counts for little. Benjamin Schwartz, in a recent study (*The World of Thought in Ancient China*, Cambridge, Massachusetts and London, Harvard University Press, 1985) has demonstrated how misleading this picutre is. As he points out, 'There are no concerns more central to Confucianism than the concern with the ethical gap between norms and actualities or the concern with the capacity of human moral agents to bridge the gap' (p. 418). According to Chinese thought, therefore, the individual necessarily has an autonomous individual life of his own distinct from the 'whole' socio-political order, which, without intervention by individuals, cannot preserve its own norms. Further, ' . . . the Chinese optimistic faith in the power of humans to shape human destiny' (p. 414) is much less evident in the pre-modern West.

60 See also chapter 1, page 18.
61 The point may be expressed, using the terminology of a standard contemporary textbook (Leif Johansen, *Public Economics*, Amsterdam and Oxford, North Holland/New York, American Elsevier, 1965) as follows. Let society consist of two individuals A and B. Assume that a given total national income R is available for private consumption by A and B (denoted by X and Y respectively) or for their joint consumption (denoted by G) to satisfy a collective want for defence. Let the utility functions for the two individuals be $U_A (X, G)$ and $U_b (Y, G)$ and let W be the social welfare function. The answer to the question of what optimally G should be, is given by maximizing W subject to the resource constraint $X + Y + G = R$; but it will vary with the way W is specified. The 'standard' specification is

$$W = W(U_A, U_B). \tag{1}$$

If the ruling authorities ascribe to defence a value beyond that ascribed by individuals we may have

$$W = W (U_A, U_B, G). \tag{2}$$

If 'social welfare' is given an *entirely* authoritarian interpretation, we have

$$W = W (X, Y, G). \tag{3}$$

We suspect that Adam Smith's view of the utility of defence veered, somewhat ambiguously, between (1) and (2).

62 The problem Weber was considering was the emigration of seasonal labour from Poland to work on farms in East Prussia. Because of large-scale migration to other parts of Germany to join the ranks of the industrial work force the region faced an acute shortage of agricultural labour. Nevertheless Weber's solution was a total ban on any further immigration of people of Polish origin together with the partitioning of large landed estates in the region into small farms, which would not produce for the market in any significant degree, and would be largely self-sufficient in respect of the demand for labour. This would, in his view, lead to a considerable reduction in agricultural output, but it would help preserve

racial purity and thereby serve the interests of the German nation state, which were paramount. (See W. J. Mommsen, *The Age of Bureaucracy, Perspectives on the Political Sociology of Max Weber*, Oxford, Basil Blackwell, 1974, p. 26–9). His position derived from the belief that the immigrants belonged to a racially inferior stock; it was only the German people 'who transformed the Poles into human beings'. (Mommsen, *The Age of Bureaucracy*, p. 33). Elsewhere, Weber wrote 'it is not peace and happiness that we shall have to hand over to our descendants but rather the principle of eternal struggle for the survival and the higher breeding of our national species' (see Mommsen, *The Age of Bureaucracy*, p. 30. See also Reinard Bendix, *Max Weber An Intellectual Portrait*, London, Heinemann, 1960, p. 43; and Anthony Giddens, *Politics and Sociology in the Thought of Max Weber*, London, Macmillan, 1972). This nationalist/racist perspective was not, as some of Weber's apologists have half-heartedly suggested, a momentary aberration but central to an understanding of Weber's sociological writings, *The Religion of China*, and *The Religion of India* in particular.

The influence of Weber may partly account for the distorted view of 'non-European' religions characteristic of sociological writing on economic development. A recent example is the grading of countries by type of religion by Adelman and Morris in their influential book, *Economic Growth and Social Equity in Developing Countries* (California, Stanford University Press, 1973). The grades A, B and C are defined as follows: 'A. Countries in which the predominant religion emphasizes the individual's responsibility for his actions and his ability to influence his environment. B and C. Countries in which the predominant religion promotes moderately fatalistic attitudes towards man's capacity to alter his destiny' (pp. 38–9). Accordingly Adelman and Morris give a C to countries with a Buddhist or Hindu population, a B to those with a Muslim population and an A⁺ to those with a mixed Christian or Jewish population. Such views rest more on suspicion than on science. I have discussed some of the issues involved in 'India's cultural values and economic development: A comment', *Economic Development and Cultural Change*, October 1964; and in *Economic Theory and the Developing Countries*, London, Macmillan, 1974, chapter 1.

63   That racist doctrines played a crucial role in determining immigration policies in Canada, Australia, New Zealand and South Africa is clearly demonstrated by Robert A. Huttenback in *Racism and Empire*, Ithaca and London, Cornell University Press, 1976. The influence of racism on immigration laws in the USA is touched on by N. R. Pole in *The Pursuit of Equality in American History*, Berkeley, University of California Press, 1978, pp. 242–3; that in Britain is briefly discussed in I. N. Stevens and D. C. M. Yardley, *The Protection of Liberty*, Oxford, Basil Blackwell, 1982, chapter 3.

64   An obvious example is the Star Wars programme; see E. P. Thompson (ed.), *Star Wars*, Harmondsworth, Penguin Books, 1985.

65 See especially his Inaugural Lecture at the University of Lund, delivered on 16 September 1904, on 'Ends and means in economics', (in Knut Wicksell, *Selected Papers on Economic Theory*, London, Allen and Unwin, 1958). The 'more or less temporary geographical boundaries of states' (ibid. p. 63) did not according to Wicksell, properly define the society whose welfare economics should be concerned with. The goal was to improve the average material conditions of humanity as a whole, i.e. of all persons, 'of whatever class of society, race, sex, language, or faith they may be' (p. 66).

Chapter 4 Application to Some Specific Indicators

1 R. S. Schofield, 'Dimensions of illiteracy, 1750–1850', *Explorations in Economic History*, vol. 11, 1973, p. 453.

2 Michael Sanderson, 'Literacy and social mobility in the Industrial Revolution in England', *Past and Present*, no. 56, August 1972; *Education, Economic Change and Society in England 1780–1870*, London, Macmillan, 1983.

3 Schofield, *Explorations in Economic History*, p. 452.

4 Cf. Sanderson's conclusion that 'the English Industrial Revolution cannot be seen as one nourished by rising educational standards at least at the elementary level' ('Literacy and social mobility in the Industrial Revolution in England', *Past and Present*, no. 56, August 1972, p. 102.

5 Lawrence Stone, 'Literacy and education in England, 1640–1900', *Past and Present*, no. 42, February 1969, p. 92.

6 The progress of literacy in France is described in R. D. Anderson, *Education in France 1848–1870*, Oxford, Clarendon Press, 1975. Social influences on the spread of literacy are lucidly discussed in Francois Furet and Jacques Ozouf, *Reading and Writing, Literacy in France from Calvin to Jules Ferry*, Cambridge, Cambridge University Press and Paris, Editins de la Maison des Sciences de l'Homme, 1982.

7 C. E. Beeby, *The Quality of Education in Developing Countries*, Cambridge, Massachusetts, Harvard University Press, 1966.

8 Some basic conceptual problems involved in the rate of return approach to education are examined in Tapas Majumdar, *Investment in Education and Social Choice*, Cambridge, Cambridge University Press, 1983.

9 Mark Blang, *An Introduction to the Economics of Education*, Harmondsworth, Penguin, 1972, p. 20.

10 Adam Smith, *An Inquiry into the Nature and Causes of the Wealth of Nations*, vol. 2, Oxford, Clarendon Press, 1976, p. 788.

11 These and other aspects of literacy regarded as a basic need are discussed in Brian Stock, *The Implications of Literacy*, Princeton, Princeton University Press, 1983; and Michael Walzer, *Spheres of Justice*, Oxford, Basil Blackwell, 1983, pp. 201–4.

12   Partha Dasgupta, *The Control of Resources*, Oxford, Basil Blackwell, 1982, p. 108.

13   Amy Gutmann, 'What's the use of going to school?' in Amartya Sen and Bernard Williams (eds), *Utilitarianism and Beyond*, Cambridge, Cambridge University Press and Paris, Editions de la Maison des Sciences de l'Homme, 1982.

14   Early Greece and Gupta-age India could be cited as examples.

15   Quoted in Lawrence Stone, 'Literacy and education in England 1640–1900', *Past and Present*, no. 42, February 1969, p. 84.

16   Thomas Laqueur, 'The cultural origins of popular literacy in England, 1500–1850', *Oxford Review of Education*, vol. 2, no. 3, 1977, p. 270.

17   During its Long March, the Chinese Red Army made a concerted and very successful effort to spread literacy among peasants who lived in areas along its line of march; the eradication of illiteracy in Cuba and Vietnam owe much to the same revolutionary tradition.

18   Robert Pattison, *On Literacy*, Oxford, Oxford University Press, 1982.

19   'The mobs of Teheran or the guerilla bands of the PLO contain large numbers of readers and writers, if we can trust the statistics for these populations. Their mechanical skills have not served to temper their cultural predispositions' (p. 128).

20   Cf. 'It is a curious fact that the mainland of Europe has never at any time produced an original system of writing, either of the more primitive, ideographic kind, or of the phonetic. This complete absence of invention is the more striking when we look at the relative abundance of systems which arose in the Eastern Mediterranean and on the shores about it', A. C. Moorhouse, *Writing and the Alphabet*, London, Cobbett Press, 1946, p. 21; see also Oswyn Murray, *Early Greece*, Sussex, The Harvester Press and New Jersey, Humanities Press, 1984, pp. 92–6.

21   See chapter 2, section 2.2.

22   Such an assumption underlies arguments made in several of the essays in Harvey J. Graff (ed.), *Literacy and Social Development in the West; A reader*, Cambridge, Cambridge University Press, 1980.

23   See William Cummings, *Education and Equality in Japan*, Princeton, Princeton University Press, 1980; and R. P. Dore, *Education in Tokugawa Japan*, London, Routledge and Kegan Paul, 1965, especially chapter X.

24   Laqueur, *Oxford Review of Education*, p. 267.

25   UNESCO, *Medium-term Plan (1977–82)*, Paris, UNESCO, 1977, Para 6116(a).

26   They are well represented in the reference given in note 22. A more balanced view can be found in Walter J. Ong, *Orality and Literacy, The technology of the word*, London and New York, Methuen, 1982.

27   E. Verne, 'Literacy and industrialization, The dispossession of speech', in Graff, *Literacy and Social Development in the West*.

28   E. P. Thompson, *The Making of the English Working Class*, Harmondsworth, Penguin, 1977, p. 347.

29 Peter Laslett's introduction to E. A. Wrigley (ed.), *Introduction to English Historical Demography*, London Weidenfeld and Nicholson, 1966, p. 4.
30 D. E. C. Eversley's introduction to Charles Creighton, *A History of Epidemics in Britain*, 2nd edn, London, Cass, 1965, p. 38.
31 See for example, Jonathan Glover, *Causing Death and Saving Lives*, Harmondsworth, Penguin, 1977, especially pp. 54–5; T. G. Roupas, 'The value of life', *Philosophy and Public Affairs*, vol. 7, no. 2, 1978; Dan W. Brock, 'The value of prolonging human life', *Philosophical Studies*, vol. 50, 1986, pp. 401–28.
32 Brock, 'The value of prolonging human life', Reference 31, p. 417.
33 A competent survey is provided in Gavin H. Mooney, *The Valuation of Human Life*, London and Basingstoke, Macmillan, 1977.
34 Dan Usher, *The Measurement of Economic Growth*, New York, Columbia University Press, 1980.
35 John Broome, 'Trying to value a life', *Journal of Public Economics*, vol. 9, 1978, pp. 91–100. Broome's position is criticized by James M. Buchanan and Roger L. Faith, 'Trying again to value a life', *Journal of Public Economics*, vol. 12, 1979, pp. 245–8 and by M. W. Jones-Lee, 'Trying to value a life' (ibid., pp. 249–56), but they add little to the argument beyond re-stating the conventional wisdom (that compensation of some sort is always possible), as duly noted by Broome in his reply 'Trying to value A life, A reply', *Journal of Public Economics*, vol. 12, 1978, pp. 259–62.
36 Thus, asserts M. W. Flinn, 'In the twentieth century, and more particularly since the Second World War, the widespread diffusion of efficient techniques of preventive and curative medicine has led to sharp reductions of death rates in underdeveloped countries that have little or no causal relationship with any economic growth that may or may not occur simultaneously', *The Origins of the Industrial Revolution*, London, Methuen, 1966, p. 19. Similarly, H. J. Habakkuk states that, compared to past European experience, recent decline of mortality in developing countries ' . . . has been much more the result of an external factor – public health improvement. The fall in death rates, is more purely autonomous in character – less directly the result of general economic and social changes and more the result of the importation of foreign medical knowledge and medical techniques', *Population Growth and Economic Development since 1950*, Leicester, Leicester University Press, 1972, p. 84. Such opinions by experts have often been echoed by journalists, politicians and authors of UN documents. A well-known UN publication, *The Determinants and Consequences of Population Trends*, vol. I, New York, 1973, asserts: 'Though the incidence or mortality during the first year of life has been considered one of the most sensitive indicators of the general level of living, being particularly sensitive to changes in environmental and social conditions, recent trends in developing countries seem to be diminishing its usefulness in this respect' (p. 123).
37 Habakkuk, *Population Growth*, reference 36.

38　Habakkuk, *Population Growth*, p. 85.
39　William Petersen, *Population*, New York, Macmillan, 1969, p. 576.
40　Reference 30, p. 39.
41　See Lado T. Ruzicka and Harald Hansluwka, 'Mortality transition in south and east Asia: Technology confronts poverty', *Population and Development Review*, vol. 8, no. 3, September 1982.
42　These are discussed in my paper 'Underdevelopment, past and present – Some comparisons of pre-industrial levels of living', Part II, *The Indian Economic and Social History Review*, vol. XVI, no. 1. See also Samuel H. Preston, *Mortality Patterns in National Populations*, New York, Academic Press, 1976, pp. 80–2.

Chapter 5 An Empirical Analysis

1　See Milton Gilbert and I. B. Kravis, *An International Comparison of National Products and Purchasing Power Currencies*, Paris, OECD, 1954; and I. B. Kravis, A. W. Heston and R. Summers, *International Comparisons of Real Product and Purchasing Power*, Baltimore, The Johns Hopkins Press, 1978.
2　For details see M. S. Ahluwalia, N. G. Carters, H. B. Chenery and Development Policy Staff, 'Growth and poverty in developing countries', World Bank Staff Working Paper no. 309 (revised), Washington DC, 1979.
3　In some cases the two sources give different figures, but the differences involved are small.
4　In its statistical reports, the World Bank classifies countries into five categories, namely low-income economies, middle-income economies, high-income oil exporters, industrial market economies and East European non-market economies. The expression 'developing countries' is normally applied to countries belonging to the first two categories although some members of the second category (Portugal, South Africa, Yugoslavia, Greece, Israel) are generally excluded, while some writers would also include countries of the third group, such as Libya and Saudi Arabia. Of the combined population in 1982 of all countries of the first two categories, as given in the *World Development Report*, 1984, the countries listed in our table 5.1 accounted for 78 per cent.
5　Spearman's rank correlation coefficient between the ordering by life expectancy at birth and the reverse rank ordering by infant mortality was 0.91.
6　At a level of significance of 1 per cent, excepting for one, which was significant at 5 per cent. Whether statistical tests of significance are at all applicable to observations of this kind, which do not constitute a random sample, is, however, open to doubt. On this point, see John Hicks, *Causality in Economics*, New York, Basic Books, 1979, especially pp. 121-2.
7　This figure is for 1959 and is taken from Gary S. Fields, *Poverty, Inequality*

and Development, Cambridge, Cambridge University Press, 1980, table 4.3, p. 65.

8 See Ajit K. Dasgupta, *Economic Theory and the Developing Countries*, London, Macmillan, 1974, p. 99.

9 See, for example, Amartya Sen, *Levels of Poverty: Policy and change*, World Bank Staff Working Paper, no. 401, 1980.

10 John Hicks has pointed out some conceptual difficulties involved in conventional statistical analysis when the observations are on entities such as different countries, localities or industries and we have relevant information about such entities that we have chosen, by our procedure, to ignore: 'By all means let us plot the points on a chart, and try to explain them; but it does not help in explaining them to suppress their names. The probability calculus is no excuse for forgetfulness' (*Causality in Economics*, New York, Basic Books, 1979, p. 122).

11 Some discussion of these can be found in André Lestage, *Literacy and Illiteracy*, Paris, UNESCO, 1982, and in references cited there.

12 All the negative coefficients, as well as some of the positive ones, are statistically insignificant; but see n. 6.

13 Indeed, according to our figures, even some countries with negative growth rates show considerable improvement in literacy and life expectancy. Too much should not however be read into this, for these growth rates were computed from the levels in the initial and terminal years only.

14 A desultory review of some aspects of the relationship is contained in Carlo M. Cipolla (ed.), *The Fontana Economic History of Europe*, London and Glasgow, Collins/Fontana, 1973, vols 3 and 4.

15 This literature is briefly discussed in Ajit K. Dasgupta, 'Under-development, past and present – Some comparisons of pre-industrial levels of living', Parts I and II, *The Indian Economic and Social History Review*, vol. XV, no. 1, 1980 and vol. XVI, no. 1, 1981.

16 Cf.: ' . . . no unambiguous rise in the standards of living of workers has been observed in any industrializing country or region before 1850.' Joel Mokyr, *Industrialization in the Low Countries 1795–1850*, New Haven and London, Yale University Press, 1976, p. 218.

17 See A. Armengaud, 'Population in Europe 1700–1914', in Carlo M. Cipolla (ed.), *The Fontana Economic History of Europe*, vol. 3, London and Glasgow, Fontana, 1973, chapter 1.

18 These figures are derived from column 6 of table 5.24, and Paul Bairoch, 'Europe's gross national product 1800–1975', *Journal of European Economic History*, vol. 5, no. 2, Fall 1976, table 6, p. 286.

19 This will be apparent to any reader of E. J. Mishan, *The Cost of Economic Growth*, London, Staples Press, 1967. See also H. W. Arndt, *The Rise and Fall of Economic Growth*, Melbourne, Longman Cheshire, 1978.

20 Both in housing and in education, decisions by public authorities (especially the State) were crucial. The importance of housing in bringing about higher levels of living in Sweden has been emphasized by K. G.

Hildebrand, who expresses his agreement with British scholars that 'better wages cannot be expected to lead to better health and significant advances in well-being until workers' housing is improved', in Peter Mathias and M. M. Postan (eds), *Cambridge Economic History*, vol. VII, part 1, p. 604). In Sweden around the end of the nineteenth century, housing accounted for 42 per cent of aggregate investment in fixed assets (twice as much as the share taken by manufacturing and mining) and public services for another 10 per cent, while in no year during the last two decades of the century did the share of housing in total investment fall below 40 per cent (ibid, p. 604). During industrialization in Britain, as we noted in chapter 1, improvement in housing conditions and environmental sanitation was long delayed. The political influence of doctrines of laissez-faire may have contributed to this delay. Peter Medawar writes: '*The Times* appeared to think that dying in one's own way without governmental interference was an elementary democratic privilege, for in an editorial on the proposal to lay a main sewer in London, *The Times* commented: "We prefer to take our chance of cholera and the rest than to be bullied into health. England wants to be clean, but not cleaned by Chadwick"' (*The Limits of Science*, Oxford, Oxford University Press, 1986, p. 20). Jeffrey Williamson, *Did British Capitalism Breed Inequality*, Boston, London and Sydney, Allen and Unwin, 1985, also has some interesting things to say on the causes of the slow pace of rise in standards of living during the Industrial Revolution in Britain, especially the impact of wars on the standard of living, though, like other contributors to this debate, he gives too much importance to the question whether there was an actual *deterioration*. How the rate of improvement in levels of living during British industrialization compares with that elsewhere is hardly discussed in the literature at all.

Arguing against the 'conventional view on the contribution of the State to economic growth', Charles B. Blankart writes: 'In the 19th century, too, governments' contribution to the growth of social overhead capital, and thereby to overall economic growth, seems to have been modest.' ('The contribution of public choice to public utility economics – A survey', in J. Finsinger (ed.), *Public Sector Economics*, London and Basingstoke, The Macmillan Press, 1983, pp. 160–1). If we are concerned with improvements in the standard of living rather than only with economic growth, the contribution of the State cannot be written off so easily.

21   Simon Kuznets, 'Underdeveloped countries and the pre-industrial phase in the advanced countries', *Proceedings of the World Population Conference*, vol. 5, 1954, p. 958. A more moderate claim is made in his *Modern Economic Growth*, 1965, table 7.5, pp. 396–7. Such claims are examined in some detail in the reference given in note 15.

22   Paul Bairoch, 'Europe's gross national product, 1800–1975', *Journal of European Economic History*, vol. 5, no. 2, Fall 1976, p. 278. See also Paul Bairoch, *The Economic Development of the Third World Since 1900*, London,

Methuen, 1975.

23 A recent exposition of this view is by Priyatosh Maitra, *The Mainspring of Economic Development*, New York, St Martin's Press, 1980.

24 Ian M. D. Little, *Economic Development*, New York, Basic Books, 1982, p. 219.

25 Paul Bairoch, *The Economic Development of the Third World since 1900*, London, Methuen, 1975, p. 187.

26 Peter Medawar, 'On the effecting of all things possible', *Pluto's Republic*, Oxford, Oxford University Press, 1982, p. 339.

27 Some is given in Little, *Economic Development*, which also gives further references.

Index

and improved facilities 113–14, 116–17
individual preferences, 109–11
monetary valuation, 111–12
and quality of life 110–11, 114–15
see also levels of living
literacy 1, 45
empirical analysis 119–31 *passim*, 134–6, 138–9, 141–4, 149–50
as social indicator 3, 96–108; and civilization 101–2; culture specific effects 104–5; individual preferences 99–101; instrumental view of 96, 99, 102–4; oral skills lost 105–8; role of 96–9; and social control 98–9, 102, 103–4
see also education
Little, I. M. D. 59, 61, 91, 93, 169
living standards *see* levels of living
Lukes, S. 37

Mack, J. 66, 69
Mahabharata 5
Malinvaud, E. 178
malnutrition 56
see also food as basic need
Malthus, T. 115
Mandel, E. 187
Mandeville, B. 18, 179
market mechanism *see* laissez-faire
Marshall, A. 25–6, 181
Marx, K./Marxism 31, 118
on basic needs 187
on British capitalism 167
on economic behaviour as social behaviour 28

on socialism 13, 88
on stage of development 22
on Third World 169
Medawar, P. 21, 174, 198
medicine *see* health care
mentalism, 38
merit goods 84–9
Mesopotamia 45, 184
migration 47, 93, 182, 191–2
military power 91–4
Mill, J. S. 34
Milton, J. 54
minimum, decent, right to 74–5
minorities 95, 107, 191–2
excellence 86
rights 82
misreading of texts 6–7
Mitchell, B. R. 156, 157
modernization *see* economic growth
monetary valuation of life prolongation 111–12
Monod, J. 21
moods 40
Moorhouse, A. C. 194
morality
and altruism 18
and basic needs 58, 71, 72
and individual preferences 36–7
of rights 73–4, 76, 80, 81, 84
mores producing norms 31
Morris, C. T. 90
mortality rates 108–9, 112–13, 115, 195
see also infant/child mortality; life expectancy
Muslims and women 129–30

nationalism 91–4
natural selection 20–1
Near East 45, 184, 194